CHOOSING HOPE
FINDING
JOY

A JOURNEY THROUGH
TRAUMA AND LOSS

By

SHERI MCGUINNESS

Choosing Hope, Finding Joy
Copyright © 2016 by SHERI MCGUINNESS
All rights reserved.

Books by Sheri McGuinness are available for
sale through Amazon.com

This book was written to help others see how grief and
trauma may have affected or could be affecting their lives.
This book does not claim to be nor should it be used in
place of seeking professional help.

Some names have been omitted to protect the
privacy of certain individuals.

Sheri McGuinness
Visit my website at www.SheriMcGuinness.com

Printed in the United States of America
First Printing: June 2016
Published by Sojourn Publishing, LLC

ISBN: 978-1-62747-216-6
EBook ISBN: 978-1-62747-217-3

TESTIMONIALS

Choosing Hope, Finding Joy *is an intimate and powerful story about the resilience of the human spirit. This true story of loss and trauma is a page-turner. It is authentically shared to assist others reclaim balance and peace in their own lives. I read it in one sitting and recommend the inspiring words of Sheri McGuinness to be a model for reclaiming joy after the heartbreak of multiple life tragedies. It gives hope to the reader that meaning and purpose can be forged from devastating loss. It reminds us that there is in each of us that same indomitable essence that encourages us to choose hope, and to find joy.*

Iris Bolton
Director Emeritus,
The Link Counseling Center NRC
Author, My Son, My Son and
Voices of Hope and Healing

With honesty and courage Sheri McGuinness invites us into some of the most difficult years of her life and allows us to walk with her as she relives both her excruciating losses and her brave journey to healing. The simplicity of Sheri's style of writing serves her challenging topics well; it undercuts the terrible tragedy of her traumas with everyday details and emotions that remind us that we, too, might have walked in her shoes. The value of this book, however, shines in Sheri's decisions not to give up and her clear descriptions of what helped her keep going. Chock full of resources and information about how to locate them, Sheri's story reminds us of the resiliency of the human spirit and the important role of personal and professional support in helping us make our way though life's dark times. This book also reinforces the power that comes from finding the words to tell one's story and demonstrates that while we may not have a choice in the way our life story unfolds; we do have the ability to write our own ending.

Maureen Underwood, L.C.S.W.
Clinical Director/Trainer
Society for the Prevention of
Teen Suicide

TABLE OF CONTENTS

Once you
Choose Hope,
Everything is
possible!

Much Love & Healing,
Sheri

DEDICATION

This book is dedicated first to my son Bobby, whose spirit guided me back to my heart and soul, and reminded me that being true to who I am is my gift to all those around me as well as to myself. He loved me unconditionally, as I did him, and he valued and respected the wisdom that I had to share – such a rare commodity to be found in young people today. He was an amazing young man and I miss him. His spirit guides me every day to stay on the path to be authentic, follow my heart and always believe!

This book is also dedicated to my other three kids: Joe, Katie and Susie who have been on this challenging journey with me for so many years; but who, after losing

Bobby, held me up when I couldn't stand and never left my side. They are unlike this "every man for himself" world; rather, they are the most loving, selfless humans I know. They have the greatest hearts, the capacity to stand strong, and the ability to let each other lean when needed. I am blessed to call them my children, and honored to call them my friends.

And lastly, this book is dedicated to my husband Joe, my soul mate and friend, who sat scouring his Bible in the early morning hours before his death. I guess we will never know exactly what his thoughts were, but he had clearly been searching for answers to be found there. He had circled several verses, and left one particular page open for us to find lying next to him. It spoke to our hearts:

And you now therefore have sorrow, but I will see you again, and your heart will rejoice.

John 16:22

INTRODUCTION

It's kind of scary to share the details of your life with the world – sometimes details that you have never shared with anyone before. But as I wrote *Choosing Hope, Finding Joy,* I knew that some of the pieces of my story were important to share with you in order to help you see just how all of the puzzle-pieces of our life experiences make up who we are today. Even if we have healed and moved on to a healthier place, these are things that are still a culmination of how we got here, and sometimes they explain why we made the choices we did along the way – good or bad.

I am not a psychiatrist, psychologist or therapist. I am just a person who has lived through a lot of tragedy and challenges. My story isn't so different than many others you may hear.

I share it with you in hopes that if you identify with me, you will see that there is a path to change things that may be negatively affecting your life. My wish is that my story may even help you find your way to a healthy and happy life.

I felt drawn to speak my truths to you, not only for my own healing but, in case you are one of those people affected by trauma. And if you see yourself reflected in some of these stories, I hope that you will recognize that some trauma responses are not normal, and not healthy – and hopefully, that you will even reach out for help.

So many people have had a loss similar to how my kids and I lost Joe; more people than you would probably think. In 2014, there were more than 42,000 suicides in our nation, and over 33,000 of them were men.

But when it happens to *your* family, you feel like the only one in the world. Suicide loss is a particularly challenging one to navigate, and although many things are similar in our losses, there is uniqueness to our lives, which brings uniqueness to our losses.

Everyone's journey is his or her own. This story is about mine. I remember so well that feeling of falling. Free falling with no vision of the ground below, just air blowing by me as I tumbled out of control for days, weeks, and even years. Having no real sense of where my children and I would land – or if we would be okay – just continually moving. Some people's faith is shaken by a loss like this, but if I hadn't held on to mine with both hands, I would have never survived. This is a story about keeping moving and trusting the path even when hopelessness sets in. It's a story of recognizing trauma and how a foundation of resilience can make the difference between survival and its alternative. It's a story of faith, and how it can keep you moving even when you can't see the path.

CHAPTER 1
HOW COULD IT BE?

Running in the door from a long workday, I drop my skirt to the ground in one zip, quickly slipping on my jeans, while all the while scanning the floor for my comfy shoes, my frantic pace interrupted by the sound of the doorbell. "Ding Dong!" I heard the sound and thought, "Who in the world could that be? I have to get on the road." As I ran to the front door, I yelled down the basement steps, "Joey, are you ready?"

As the words left my lips, I cringed. He had wanted me to call him Joe from the moment he hit fourteen, but five years later I still struggled to think of him as Joe. He had always been our Joey. His dad was Joe. I just couldn't find a compromise – Big Joe, Little Joe: Joe Sr., Joe Jr. – so I kept slipping. Without even a hint of annoyance, "I'm coming Mom," came the response from below. He knew it wasn't the moment to chastise Mom. I turned the corner, and as I reached for the doorknob, I had no idea that what was on the other side of the door would change our world forever.

I had gotten up early that morning; my husband Joe had stayed at his buddy Pete's house the night before, as he did sometimes, for a "boy's night." He never drove after he drank, not even two beers. He had learned that lesson many years before. So he always just spent the night at his buddy's when that was the case.

After getting myself up early, showered and mostly dressed, I hustled the three youngest out of bed, creating definite movement before heading to the kitchen to get breakfast going and make school lunches. My twin girls, Katie and Susie were ten. They were the easy ones to get going. Twelve-year-old Bobby, on the other hand, was another story. After much hustle and bustle, with everyone fed, they grabbed their lunches, then a kiss on the head and out the door. "Oh," remembering as I stuck my head out the window, "Don't forget, I will be home by 5:30. See you all then. I love you – and make it a great day!!" I always told them to make it a great day, making it clear that it was always in their power to be happy with themselves and their choices as they went through each day.

As I saw them climb the stairs of the bus, it seemed as though everyone had gotten out with little drama. That made it a good day for me! After years of taking care of my little ones, having home-based daycare and any other job that I could do and still be home with them, today was my first day at a new part-time job outside of the house. I was nervous and excited at the prospect. Glancing at myself in the mirror, I straightened my collar and smoothed my hair, and as I looked at my reflection a smile grew across my face. Thoughts of possibilities raced through my head, as I was about to embark on this new chapter. The kids were finally old enough to be in the house alone for the hour that it would take for me to get home after work, and we really needed the money. Joe had been having some serious struggles, and this additional income would take the pressure off of us.

I picked up my purse and my keys and headed to the door. Before I could reach the knob, the phone rang. Darting back to the kitchen, I stumbled to get the phone before it went to voice mail. "Hello," I said, breathing hard as the voice on the other end responded. "Hi, this is Julie from Reliable, and we were just wondering if Joe will be coming into work after he picks up his mother at the airport?"

The phone filled with silence as I contemplated how to answer that. I knew I would be picking up Joe's mom much later that night. She was flying in for a visit from

California. We hadn't seen her in quite a while. But Joe wasn't picking her up. So why was she asking this question? What was he up to? I quickly responded, "I'm not sure, Julie, but I will have him call you as soon as I speak with him." She said "Thank you," and I hurriedly hung up and began to dial Joe. It went straight to his voice mail. My face tightened with an annoyed look, scrunching my eyes and mouth. Maybe they had "too much fun" last night and he felt like a day off, but he usually would pick up for me no matter what. With all Joe had been going through, this call would have been worrisome, but for the past couple of weeks, Joe had seemed better. He had spent special time with each of the kids, giving glimpses of the Dad he had always been. I had felt some relief, as if we might have turned a corner with his struggles. For a moment, I contemplated heading to Pete's to make sure everything was okay, but I decided that Joe was probably sleeping, and that I would just keep trying him throughout the day. I knew that I couldn't be late for my first day at the new job. So I headed off to work.

It was such a busy day. There was so much to learn, and the day seemed to give no pause. Once it finally ended I gave him a ring, but still no answer. All of a sudden, I felt sick in the pit of my stomach. I couldn't decide whether to be mad or scared. I jumped in my car and headed home, anxiously trying him again and again. Finally I decided to call Pete.

Pete answered instantly, but he acted very strange. I said, "Where is he, Pete, what's going on?" Speaking very slowly and concisely, he said, "Sheri, he's not here, I promise you, he's not here." It was clear that these were carefully chosen words. But they didn't convince me. I knew something wasn't right, and I had to go find Joe to see for myself what was going on, no matter what trouble he may have gotten himself into this time. We had been through plenty of challenges in life, and I always took them head on. I called home and my son Joe answered. I asked if Dad was there, and he said no. I told him briefly what was going on, and to get ready, and that I would be right there to get him to ride with me to Pete's house to see if we could figure this out. When I reached home, I barely had time to run in and change when the doorbell rang. As I gripped the handle and swung open the door, my heart sank. The sight of the Cherokee County sheriff standing before me was not what I imagined or wanted to see.

He was a dark-haired man of about my age, a pleasant-looking guy with a slip of paper in his hand. He very politely asked if I was Mrs. McGuinness, and I replied yes. He said, "I was told to deliver this note to you." I took it from his hand, and sensed that he didn't know what it was all about. I asked him to come in, closing the door behind him. By now, my son Joe had made it up the stairs, and the other three kids had come into the room – all of them wondering why a police officer was at our door. As I read the telephone number out loud, I questioned where the exchange might be from. The officer jumped in to say, "Oh, I think that's DeKalb Medical Center; my wife works there." Such fear came over me, even as he spoke those words. I knew he was hoping to reassure me that maybe Joe was in the hospital rather than dead. I dialed the number, and waited for a voice.

After four rings, a machine answered my call. The voice of a sweet young lady said, "DeKalb Coroners Office. We are unable to answer your call, please leave a message and we will get back to you as soon as possible." As her words hit my ears, I let out a gasp, making it clear to the whole room that this was not good. I left a message and as I hung up the phone, I glanced up with a look of horror.

We were all in disbelief that we had to wait for a return call. Those minutes seemed like hours until the phone finally rang. It was the same sweet voice that I had heard on the machine. She asked me please to hold for the coroner.

When I heard his voice, I am sure he probably said his name, but all I remember was him saying, "I am so sorry to tell you, Mrs. McGuinness, that your husband Joe died at 2 pm today from a single, self-inflicted gunshot wound to the head". I looked up at my son Joe, the tears running down my face, and said, "He did it Joe, he's gone."

CHAPTER 2
THE RUBBLE OF SUICIDE

I could barely breathe, let alone speak. My chest felt as though it had a hundred-pound brick on it. I had always been a proactive, "we can handle anything" kind of gal. But all I could think was, there's nothing I can do: no finding a solution; no making a plan; no second chances. The decision had been made – and there was no turning back.

In just those few seconds after hearing those life-changing words, my mind raced and ran through the last few days, moment by moment, with lightning speed; thoughts darting from one picture to the next like a reel from an old-time movie, looking for signs of what had gone wrong. How could I be so stupid? How did I not know? How could I have thought that he was better? What is wrong with me! My thoughts were quickly interrupted by the coroner's voice. "Joe left a note for you, Sheri," he said. "DeKalb County Sheriff's Department has told me that it could be released to you, and you can pick it up any time after one o'clock tomorrow."

As I hung up the phone, I whisked the kids to their rooms, thinking I had to protect them from hearing this devastating news. I don't know why. What was I thinking? Somehow I wanted to save them from what was about to happen to their world, but I quickly realized that I couldn't keep them in their rooms forever. There was no way for me to protect them from this, and I began to cry. Warm tears ran down my face, the salty wetness hitting my lips, as I gasped for air in between the sounds of my sobs. My son Joe came and put his arms tight around me, and I knew in that moment that we were all in this together. No matter what I did, I couldn't keep the little ones from going through this bomb exploding in their lives. We would just have to deal with it together, walking through the rubble, picking up the pieces as a family. I called each of their names and brought them back into the room, making it clear that together we would survive this.

There was no shame in the pain that their father had dealt with those last few years of his life. The pain of his past did not diminish the precious man and father that he was. He had been a wonderful, loving father who adored his kids, and they knew that he was struggling and suffering. Sitting down beside them on the couch, I clung to my babies as we tried to fathom what had just happened. They were all so young to deal with something so complex, and so very painful. My heart broke for them.

I explained what the coroner had said. The room got quiet. I think we were all in shock. In an instant, everything we ever knew to be true was changed forever. As I sat with my arms around them, weeping, I was consumed with the realization that I had failed him. This was my fault. He had been struggling for some time, and as we searched for ways to help, I was the healthy one, he was sick, and I had failed him. The image of this man I loved, in so much pain, and in such a lonely, dark place, giving up, deciding that ending his life was his only option, haunted my thinking. The pain had won. The tears poured as thoughts of his last moments ran through my mind. What was he thinking? Was he afraid, did he feel alone, had I allowed him to become hopeless, did he blame me, will the children blame me, did he wish he had another choice but just couldn't see it? I looked at the children's faces as they heard the news, their little eyes full of devastation and shock. I couldn't help wondering how we would survive this, and if we would survive this.

As I replayed the voice of the coroner speaking in my head, I plummeted into feelings of complete despair. My thoughts swirled with unending movement. The pain was so severe that I was struggling to put my own thoughts together in a way that even made any sense. What do I do next, how do we proceed, what will happen to us; so many questions and no ability to logically sort through them. Terrifying fear joined the pain as my mind began to free fall into the darkness where I could see no bottom.

The color had left the officers face as I told what the coroner had said, and it was apparent that he had no idea that they had sent him to a call with a little slip of paper and not a mention that my husband was dead. Even though the officer was upset, he did such a wonderful, caring job of helping us through those first moments. Although clearly moved, he went about trying to figure out how to best help my little family.

He gathered everyone he could think of to come to us and support us as we figured out what to do. The house began to fill with family, friends, neighbors, pastors, and more. He didn't leave until he knew we were well taken care of. The house was overflowing with support, and even then, he made sure that I knew how to reach him if I needed anything else.

I don't remember a lot of the details of what happened that day, or on many of the ones that followed. I guess that's what shock does: it protects us in that way so the pain is not as great. But honestly, I don't know how it could have hurt any more than it did.

The officer had arranged to send someone to meet my mother-in-law's plane that night. They took her to an area of the airport where they could talk to her before bringing her home to my house. I don't even remember her arriving, but I knew she was there. Looking back, I feel terrible that I wasn't much of a comfort to her. This was her son, her baby boy. I love her dearly, but

I was so consumed with grief and the children's immediate needs that I couldn't see much else.

One of the people who came out that first night was Pete. He tried his best to relay the details of the day, thinking that Joe was playing hooky from work, which he had done plenty of times in the past. Wrenched with guilt, he told me that Joe had taken his life in his apartment, with his gun. How did he not know that his friend was at the end? But none of it mattered now. We couldn't change a thing, only deal with cleaning up the rubble in the wake of the tsunami that had hit our lives.

This day was the first of many days that seemed like a fog. And it was a huge effort to get beyond each one, not knowing where life was leading us next. The children and I were traumatized and shaken to the very core, but I made the decision early on that their loving father's choice, made from great pain, would not define them for all time. I had to figure out how, and I would!

When I awoke the next morning, for a brief moment I wondered if it had all been a bad dream – but I knew better. I hadn't really slept; my mind just went over and over all that had happened the previous day. Going through the motions of what needed to be done next, I made sure trusted souls were watching my young ones as I made the necessary plans, and headed to the coroner's office.

My sister Susan, her husband Dave, my brother Bob and his wife Jane had arrived and were going to help me take care of the details. They drove me into the city to meet with the coroner. When we got there, he came out and brought the note that Joe had left for me.

I thought that they would let me see Joe, but they wouldn't. The coroner said that Joe was in no condition to be seen, and that I didn't need to have that picture in my head. I thought, "How dare he make that decision for me? This is my husband, my love, my soul mate!" He advised me that it would be better for me to see him at the funeral home, and I was too emotionally exhausted to argue with him.

But the fallout of that decision was that my mind was faced with a huge puzzle. Not being there when Joe was found left me with so many unanswered questions. Trying to put together the pieces of his last moments seemed imperative, almost obsessive. I couldn't stop thinking about it. What did his last moments look like? Where was he? Was he pacing, sitting? What had he been doing...thinking? Knowing that his Bible was found beside him, I could imagine him sitting on the edge of that bed reading it, and circling passages that would help convince him that the Lord wouldn't turn him away and that he would see us again.

But, why did he give up? Did he know how much we loved him, how much I loved him? Was he wishing I were there to hold him, to comfort him, to stop him? Was he scared? What was he thinking as he put the gun to his temple and pulled the trigger? Did he change his mind as the trigger set the bullet on its path?

I imagined the swing of his arm as the bullet left the chamber, propelling his lifeless hand and releasing the gun as it hit the ground, sending it sliding across the floor. I pictured the red wetness seeping out onto the pillow as he lay there. Why did I need these images? Why couldn't I stop the endless movie in my head as I tried to imagine what had happened? So many unanswered questions, holes in the story that my mind was desperate to fill with some kind of resolution. It seemed crazy, but I knew my mind wouldn't rest until I pieced it all together.

So instead of seeing Joe, I sat down with the coroner as he talked about the ramifications of a note from a hopeless, emotional man who was clearly on the edge of sanity. It was a long, rambling note that gave some understanding of what he was thinking, but mostly it gave me more pain. He told me that he knew I was trying to help him see that there was hope, but he no longer believed that it would ever find its way to him. This was the saddest feeling I had ever felt: that he had lost all hope, and didn't feel that he deserved a second chance. He clearly believed that this choice would relieve us of the challenges that his new struggles had brought on our family. He felt as though his illness had made him a burden. And as I read those words, I remember the breath leaving me. I prayed that this was his own perception, and that I had never made him feel that way.

The note went on and on, but much of it was the rambling and sporadic thoughts of a simple man who felt he had little to give to those he was leaving behind. His final words were, "Now you can go on..." He had no idea what that meant for the family he loved so dearly.

CHAPTER 3
THE HORRORS OF HIS PAST

Joe had tried many times to share the pain of his past. Though I didn't know what it was exactly, I had a pretty good guess. But I had never pressured him to speak it. He was clearly tortured by it, and I felt that when he was ready, he would share it with me.

In 1995, Joe's dad died. He died a gruesome death that greatly affected his family, and especially Joe. After his heart-bypass surgery, complications followed that resulted in gangrene in both legs. We hadn't gone out to California, where Dad lived, to be with him for the surgery. It was such a common procedure at that time that we decided to wait for him to get out of surgery, and we believed he was healthy enough to make it through with great results.

Unfortunately, those life changing complications ensued, and the doctors made the decision to amputate one of Dad's legs. They were also thinking about amputating the second leg. At that point, Joe and I got on the next flight out to California.

It seemed as though it took us forever to get there, and when we finally did, Dad was already in a coma. As they prepared to amputate his second leg, Dad passed away. Joe hadn't gotten to speak with him, or say goodbye. It was a hard time for the entire family, but especially for Joe.

When we came home after Dad's funeral, Joe's life began to crumble, and he was never the same. I was so confused as to why he just couldn't get his life together. I knew he would be grieving, but this seemed bigger than that. He tried so hard to get his feet under him. I think that he wasn't clear why he was falling apart either. But everyone around him could see that he was on the brink, desperately grasping to hold on to his own sanity.

Don't get me wrong; our life wasn't always perfect and then all of a sudden he had a breakdown. There were a handful of times in our years together when stress overcame him, and he did some crazy thing. It always threw me that out of the blue he would crash and burn. But it was always at a time of greatest stress.

There were clearly signs that something haunted him, and when the pressure and anxiety got overwhelming, his coping mechanisms were nonexistent. He usually leaned on drugs to sedate him. Our world would be in upheaval and we would struggle to get back to normal again, but we had long periods – years of a loving and happy life together – until life would challenge his ability to cope again.

The traumatic way that Joe's dad had died stretched his coping skills beyond their limits, and this time there was no quick fix. We tried so many things, including getting him in to see a couple of different psychiatrists, both of whom simply overmedicated him instead of helping him deal with the root cause of the problems.

I learned much later, long after Joe's death, that when you have a trauma in your later life, it can trigger an emotional reaction similar to one caused by trauma in your young life, especially if the earlier trauma had gone untreated or undertreated. It can revisit you with a vengeance, which was exactly what was going on for Joe. I didn't know that at the time – or, for that matter, any of Joe's history – so I wasn't much help in finding the right therapeutic response. But I kept trying!

We could never get past the medication to maybe get some counseling. No individual counselor would work with him to get to the bottom of the problem. They wanted him to have a certain amount of time sober before that, but he couldn't stand the pain, so he couldn't let go of the alcohol and drugs. So, I asked Joe if we could go to couples counseling. I figured that if he thought it was all about me, he would do it. And surprisingly, he said yes. The counselor that we were going to start working with sent us first to an eight-week course, which he said would open our thinking and prepare us for a good counseling experience.

It was called "Adult Children of Confusion" which started with the eight-week educational course and then moved to a support-group format. The name always made me laugh! Where did they come up with this stuff!! But it actually was an awesome class that helped me find great clarity. For Joe, though, it was a very different experience.

We went along week by week, learning so much, and clearing a lot of old, dysfunctional family choices and behaviors. It wasn't a perspective of blame, but more a look at how to step out of those old roles that didn't work, and start finding healthier ways to live. I could tell he was consuming the information, and even thriving in the group. He was beginning to understand how the circumstances of his past could influence where he was now. Many others in the class were having great revelations and healing. And as his trust built, on the last day of class, he finally found the courage to tell this group of thirty other wounded souls that he had been sexually abused from the time he was five until he was eleven.

A neighbor friend would often help the family by entertaining "wee" Joe, as they called him. This man would take little Joe to the movies or the park, spending a few hours or the day together. Joe's mom had no idea what this man was up to. The abuse had only stopped when the man finally moved away.

Until that very moment when Joe spoke those words to the group, no other human had known the devastating abuse that he had suffered in the hands of this monster.

I was crushed to think that this little guy, only five years old, had to endure these horrible atrocities. The man had threatened his life, so that if Joe told a soul of his torture, the man would kill him, and his family as well. And although, I am sure that this little guy's personality must have changed in many ways, no one figured out what was going on – no one saved him. My heart was so broken for him.

Even though I had great compassion for his horror, I didn't know what to do to help him find his way to the other side of it. We had opened a can of worms that could not be closed.

So now, at age forty, he was dealing with the raw emotions of that scared, tormented five-year-old boy. He couldn't bring himself to ever return to "face" the group again even though many of the group members had divulged similar stories. But, the shame he felt was huge.

It didn't make sense to me. It seemed that this poor little boy had been taken advantage of, abused; he had no fault in that. But it didn't have to make sense to me. These feelings were real and painful, and they were eating him alive. He had buried them so deep, for so long, and now they were like a flame that perpetually burned his skin – and no amount of water could put it out.

I tried so many ways to help Joe, but as his life broke down, so did my ability to get him to the help he so desperately needed. Joe could barely work by this point, and we lost our health insurance, so not much was available to him – especially help that cost a fortune. It took everything we had to get him mediocre care, and he was still constantly overmedicated. He fought the fight for almost four years. It was a hard four years, a scary four years, and an unsure four years that constantly teetered on the brink of disaster.

He struggled with addiction: alcohol, pain medications, even heroin – anything he could find to calm his anxiety, ease the pain and allow him to hide from the carnage of his youth. He felt so defined by this flawed persona, and certainly felt judged by those around him – most of whom only knew what was happening on the surface, and it just looked like bad behavior to them. But as harsh as those around him were in judging his outward behavior, they didn't judge him more than he judged himself. The reality was that our life had become chaos –and that was terrifying for me, dangerous for him, and frightening as I tried to protect the kids from what he was dealing with.

Oddly, during the week before his death, something seemed better. There really wasn't much going on that would have facilitated any sort of breakthrough, but I had no mental-health background, and I didn't know what to expect, so I felt good that he seemed better – maybe even as though we had turned a corner.

He spent good quality time with each of the kids that week, and his spirits were high. Another important fact that I learned, long after I lost Joe, is that when a person finally makes up their mind that suicide is their only option, they get a peace about them. Even though it's not the option that they really want, it is the only answer they can find, and they are relieved that they finally have found their answer. And that is what was going on with Joe.

He had made up his mind that there just was no other option, and he couldn't operate with this level of pain any longer. He felt that he had lost his identity, the husband and father that he had worked so hard to be, and he couldn't see hope ever finding its way to him. Joe didn't want to die; he wanted to live the way he had lived with the wife and children he loved. He tried for almost four years to find his way back, to find the answer, to find relief, but he got tired. It's hard to live long term with that level of pain, and emotional pain is often more excruciating than physical pain.

In Joe's long four-page note, much of it rambling with conscious thought slipping in and out as he pondered his last moments, he made it clear that the pain was so intense that he just couldn't bear it any longer. He had also begun to feel like a burden to the family, and he believed that he was dragging his family down. He didn't want to give up, but he just didn't believe that relief would ever be his. As I read his words, my heart broke again and again.

After all he had been through as a young boy, and even with the challenges that his past had brought to his life, he had worked so hard to love me and love his kids. And the kids loved him so dearly. He had vowed to never strike one of them. And he never did.

But that Dad, the one he had always wanted to be, was a distant memory, and the chaotic, medicated Dad who could barely function was all that he could see. His challenges had made it hard to do any of the things he had always done with the kids. And it was an enormous loss for him.

CHAPTER 4

A GENTLE FATHER, A PRECIOUS MAN

In better times, Joe was a peaceful, loving, bright, creative, caring man, and a true musician at heart. He had another trade, but he really would have preferred to be a musician full time. He was so talented.

I think about it now, and I wish somehow I had made it possible for him to be just that. However, with a house full of kids and bills to pay, working in a regular paying job just seemed like our only option. But there was never a doubt what his true calling was.

He came home every single day from work and played music. Sometimes he would play acoustic guitar, sometimes electric, sometimes bass, but he played every night. He taught every one of the children to play multiple instruments. He taught them to appreciate all music, and exposed them to a broad range of genres.

When Bobby was just a little toddler in diapers, Joe had taught him to play the drums, by sitting him in the middle of the floor with books of all sizes surrounding him. Giving him two wooden spoons, he taught him to listen for how each book had a very different sound as he struck them. After that, Bobby would come into the room with his wooden spoons and create his "drum kit" every night and play with Daddy. His skills began to far surpass his age, and he became one of the most brilliant drummers that ever played.

My twins, Katie and Susie, learned to play mandolin first and then other instruments, and they sang like beautiful songbirds, and still do. When they were very young he would let them make up words for songs, and he would put music behind it. The two little girls would stand side by side in front of him and sing the song while Daddy played. Their little cherub voices filled the air with sweet melodies and laughter. I remember one song, about little pumpkins, that he and the girls wrote together. We still have his binder where he kept every one of his writings, every song, and every note: a precious treasure.

Around the age of five, our oldest son, Joe began to show signs that he was clearly a musical child prodigy. One day while we were visiting friends, he sat down at the piano and began to play with both hands, having never played before. We were all in shock as we heard him play. I quickly got him into lessons, but the teacher told me that he had so much innate talent – and no interest in theory – that she really couldn't help him. He picked up the saxophone and taught himself, and eventually the guitar, and any other instrument that interested him. Son Joe went on to be a talented musician and songwriter with a bright future. Dad Joe was so proud of him for many reasons, but to have this prodigy as his child just made him beam with pride.

He loved to play music with his son, especially as young Joe got older – they challenged each other and pushed for excellence. But the other kids were talented also, and Joe was proud of them as well, working with them to help them learn all they could consume about music.

I know most people thought we were a little daft, because every instrument you could think of, including amplifiers and microphones, were permanent fixtures in our den. Once Bobby was ready, we bought him a full drum kit, which had a place of honor in one corner of the room, ready for action at a moment's notice. Music was always drifting through the air, filling each room in our home, whether it was Joe quietly strumming, loudly rocking, or sometimes the whole family band playing at full tilt. It was almost always loud – but most of the time it was amazing. I would be listening, and singing along in the kitchen, while I prepared dinner or made breakfast on the weekend. To watch Joe and all four kids play was a joy beyond words. It brought them and me so much pleasure.

Growing up with music as my foundation, this just felt natural. And now this was the foundation that brought my kids together. A flood of memories runs through my mind as I think of those precious times. I'll never forget one day when Joe, son Joe and I sat together trying to put together three-part harmony to "Sugar Magnolia!" We just could not get it right, and through about 200 tries, we laughed so hard.

I miss the music; it was in large part the glue that held us together. And after Joe died, our house got very quiet. And it stayed quiet for a very long time.

*Daddy and
Joey, 1981*

*Daddy and
Bobby, 1986*

*Daddy, Susie and
Katie, 1996*

CHAPTER 5
LOOKING BACK

I came from a loving family, with a great mom and dad who loved us dearly. We never really wanted for much. Maybe some individual attention would have been nice in the midst of a large family. There were five of us kids and we lived an average Norman Rockwell life, starting out in a small home with lots of shared space, to a life of abundance that my father had dedicated himself to providing for us. We were raised to work hard, have integrity in all we do, be trustworthy, and love and look after family. I learned and lived unconditional love.

There were a number of incidents that took place in my young life that were somewhat similar to what Joe had experienced. For me, it was a series of ill-fated events that happened and had left me with unrecognized and untreated scars. It wasn't consistent, ongoing abuse to the degree that Joe had endured, but enough to really alter my path.

Around the age of seven, a trusted adult in my life had broken that trust and put me in a number of inappropriate sexual situations over many years. So starting at a very young age, my norms were seriously altered. During and after that time, I seemed to become a magnet to other predators that crossed my path until I was old enough to know that I could choose not to be a victim, and be able to get myself out of a compromising situation.

I had never told a soul of the things that had happened to me. I'm not sure if I thought I had done something wrong and that I would be in trouble, or if I was told to keep a secret. Honestly, I can't remember much of the details – and that's probably a good thing. But I don't recall feeling that I was living with a secret, just very alone. It felt as though it was just part of my life.

I can see now, that my personality began to change. I became more reserved and had a hard time fitting in, making friends, and being in large groups. I do remember at around ten, wanting to end my life. I actually opened my bedroom window and was going to jump from the second story. I can't remember what stopped me, but I do remember crying myself to sleep that night.

I know now that the repercussions of not only sexual abuse but degradation as well can really change a child's inner voice, and their perception of themselves and the world around them. And because the abuse had gone unnoticed by my parents, no intervention was ever sought, so I didn't see these things as anything different than anyone else's life; and I never recognized that they had changed my life and colored my reality.

I didn't realize the impact that these events actually had until I was much older. But they definitely left me dealing with trauma issues that would change the trajectory of my life from a very early age. That trauma would distort the way I made decisions, the way I made friends and even the way I chose a partner in life. It took repeated traumas throughout my adult life for these distortions in thinking to become clear to me.

When Joe came into my world, I fell in love with him instantly. The day we met, I came into the store for a job interview, and saw him through a window to the back room. He smiled and I melted. I never really thought that way, love at first sight? I wasn't even sure what that was. But I remember the instant pull. He said that he had felt the same response.

We played cat and mouse for a while, but eventually it was just undeniable. Looking back I can see that there was incredible love that was there from the start. I believe it was a gift directly from

God, but there was also a familiarity that we had with each other that was unspoken, unacknowledged and maybe even not known. But it was a pronounced kinship of two broken souls. Beyond the instant attraction, the subliminal connection was indisputable.

Back then, I had no idea what he had actually suffered through as a child and a young boy. And it wasn't until many years later that I would find out what lay beneath the surface.

Not many people knew the real Joe: how intelligent he was, how funny, how kind, how loving – and so damn sexy. I'll never forget his lips; the way they felt in my mouth: tender, round and soft. From the first time he kissed me until the day he died, he could put his arms around me and put his lips on mine, and I would melt and run down into my shoes. It was a passionate love, connected at the core, until the very end.

Throughout our marriage, the challenges of Joe's baggage were always there. I didn't always understand what they were, but I knew there was something. Because of the challenges that Joe's struggles brought into our marriage, no one else in our life understood the connection.

It seemed black and white to them. But I learned long ago that there isn't much that is really black and white. My parents had taught me unconditional love. That is the level of love that I felt growing up, and the level of love that I offered. My mistakes were never punished with the loss of love, and I was always helped back up and made stronger by them. It became who I am, and I wouldn't ever walk away from Joe.

My love for him was the first time he ever felt love that was unconditional. It took him a long time to understand it, to believe it, to realize that it would not go away, and also to be grateful for it.

CHAPTER 6
BURYING MY MAN, OUR DREAMS AND OUR FUTURE

The details of the day Joe died were a swirl of events, emotions, activities, and people flooding to our door, holding us up, helping us survive. I barely remember being at the funeral home that week.

Joe wanted to be cremated. But the counselor had explained that before Joe was cremated, his children needed closure. So we arranged to have a visitation that allowed the kids to say goodbye.

As we arrived at the funeral home, my mind was almost numb. I knew I needed to focus on the children, getting them through this moment. One of the staff took me aside and brought me into the room where Joe had been set to receive visitors. They wanted me to make sure that everything was all right before the children went in to see him. As we walked into the room, I could see Joe's body lying in the casket. Approaching him, I remember thinking that it didn't look like my Joe. His poor face was swollen, lifeless and still. The funeral director walked into the room behind us, moving toward me and whispering in my ear. He told me that he wanted to personally hand me Joe's wedding ring. I turned and looked at his face, contemplating all that those words meant. Slowly I raised my cupped hand, shaking as I watched the ring fall from his fingers and into the palm of my hand. My sweet Joe's ring lay there; presenting the fact that not only was my Joe gone, the life with the man I loved finished, but also that my marriage was over. As my fingers curled up and tightened around the cold piece of gold, I began to sob.

Creeping my way to the restroom where I could find a moment of privacy, I reached over and locked the door behind me. Walking across the room and past the mirror, I spotted the face of a broken woman. As I leaned against the wall, the cold of the tiles penetrated my body and I started to shake. I'm not sure if it was the temperature or the realization of where the life of the woman I saw in the mirror had found its way to. My swollen, puffy face told a story, one of a fighter who was badly beaten and had lost. I had definitely lost the battle, but I knew I couldn't lose the war. My children's lives depended on it.

As I stepped out of the restroom I glanced down the long hall, seeing my children heading my way. Grabbing for my tissues, I wiped my wet face and prepared myself for a role that was still mine, to make sure these kids were going to be okay.

As they approached, I hugged and kissed each one. It was time for them to go into the visitation room and say goodbye to their dad. I walked toward the room, and guided the kids to the door. Although the boys and Katie went into the room, Susie couldn't bring herself to go in, pausing at the door jam and holding it as if to protect her from what she was about to see. She peeked from the doorway, and although I am sure that she saw him from across the room, she didn't want to enter, and that was fine. We talked with her, and the counselor was there to help each of them as they said goodbye. As hard as it was to let go of the love of my life, it was even harder to watch my children do so, and wipe the tears from their faces promising that we would all be okay – especially when I wasn't sure that we would.

I had fought so long for Joe to find help, to find hope. I had let go of our dreams long before this day. A few months earlier, the counselor we were seeing had said, "Sheri, Joe loves you and the kids so very much, and he is trying so hard to be what you need him to be. But the reality is that although it may fall short of what a healthy husband might be able to provide, he is giving you everything he has to give right now."

That was such a gift, as it really helped me get perspective. It was hard because even though I understood how much he was struggling, I didn't want the world to perceive him as coming up short. Many of those around us were judging him from a viewpoint of not knowing any of the reality of what he was dealing with. But once I grasped what the counselor had said, it made it much easier to have more appropriate expectations, and it took a lot of pressure off Joe, and off me. Then my focus turned to loving him and helping him find support.

In the midst of this chaotic life and raising children, I realized that our dreams should have been very different. I could see that our priorities were all screwed up, and based on all the wrong things. Nothing seemed so important anymore. My perspective had changed in every aspect of our lives. And so many things seemed petty and insignificant.

I was in a free fall, where moments grabbed me and I took care of life – but the reality was that I was still falling, long and fast, and it seemed like an eternity. I knew somehow in the deepest place in my heart that we would be okay, but I'm not sure where that even came from. My faith? I had always believed that if I held strong the Lord would light my path so that my steps would be steady and sure. And although I could no longer see the path, I hung on to that promise. And I trusted that if I just kept believing, one moment, one day, maybe even one year, my feet would hit the ground right where they were meant to be.

We got through the funeral and burial with the help of my family. The details had been all taken care of, but then we were left alone to figure out how we go on. How would we keep living with this huge hole in our family and in our hearts? How would we smother the pain that was a constant reminder that he was gone, and there was nothing that we could do about it?

After that first week ended and all the family and friends had gone home, the house got very quiet. So quiet... it felt like there was a heartbreaking cloud of sadness physically hanging over us. The beautiful sounds that had floated through our home each night were gone, and the silence was deafening. I ached for the noise, for the loud drumming and the chords being played through those amplifiers. For my children's voices to be striking the air mixed with his. But the denseness of this quiet air lay upon me like a heavy weight: making it hard to breathe, making it hard to think, and making it hard to be. It amplified the emptiness and echoed in the hole in my heart.

The children and I were open and we talked about it, but my pain was so deep that I was afraid to share it with them on an adult level. So I would wait and cry in my room, or I would get them off to school in the morning as happily as I could, and then I would get in my car and head to my job – and cry from the moment I left my driveway until the moment that I got to work. I know the people passing by must have thought I was crazy, but it was the only space I had where these poor broken children wouldn't see their broken-hearted mom weeping uncontrollably. I would wipe my face, go into work, and then cry all the way home again.

My son Joe was my rock. He was so strong. I wasn't purposely letting him step in for his dad, but it didn't take long for me to realize that I was treating him like a secondary adult in the house, and he really still was just a grown child who had lost his dad.

He was trying to take the pressure off me, and he had started taking the younger kids to their support group. And because I was anxious to get everyone on a healing path, I pushed him onto the same path. But he had a lot of anger and was clearly struggling. I learned very quickly that I needed to let him focus on his own grief.

But for me, I was left holding broken dreams that were forever shattered. I couldn't even think of what the future looked like – I was barely surviving the here and now.

CHAPTER 7
WHEN THE DUST SETTLED

Getting life back on track after this kind of loss is challenging at best. Most of the family and friends who had rushed to us had returned home to their own happy families, seemingly not giving a second thought to how shattered our lives were. The brokenness would impact us for years as we tried to find our footing, but for now there was just fear and isolation. We were left to pick up the pieces on our own, with no guidebook and no real support.

Most of my friends vanished, not knowing what to say or how to help. It was awkward, so they just disappeared. Sadly, many of my friends were the parents of my children's friends. So the kids lost their support system as well.

Financially, we were drowning and I didn't know how to change that. We were struggling before Joe died. Now we were in big trouble. A cloud of fear constantly hung over me, worrying that I would come home from work to the electricity or water being cut off, or a bill collector at my door, or worse. We almost lost the house, as it went into foreclosure three times in those first few years. I lived in a constant state of trauma and anxiety.

One of the times that we were served with foreclosure, two neighbors showed up at my door. As I answered the door, I heard, "Oh Sheri, we saw your house in the foreclosure listings! How can we help?" I think I was embarrassed at first, but I have to tell you, my heart was renewed. I had felt so alone for so long in all that was happening, and just that someone had noticed we were in trouble and responded with an outreached hand gave me such strength. As it turned out, that morning I had mustered up the courage to ask my brother to loan me the money to get the house out of foreclosure – which didn't eliminate the main problem, but it saved the day for that moment.

One evening, late in the middle of the night, a tow truck showed up and repossessed my Ford Expedition. He didn't knock on my door. The flashing lights from his truck through my bedroom window woke me out of a deep sleep, and I jumped to my feet. It was like trauma on top of trauma, and I couldn't get control. At three o'clock in the morning, I stood in my front yard dressed only in my nightgown, begging the man not to take my car. "Please, I have young children and no way to get around," I said. 'What will I do without my car?" But he didn't care; he was just doing his job. "Ma'am, that's between you and your finance company. Now get your crap out of the car or you will have to collect it at the repo lot next week," he said, clearly hardened by the repetition of repossessing some poor struggling soul's vehicle.

I lived with such a high level of stress for so long that my health began to suffer. I had always believed that losing a child was the worst loss that you could ever experience, and I still believe that, even though every loss is painful and we all have the right to grieve equally without measure. But one of the biggest challenges of losing your spouse is that suddenly you are alone in this mess! Even with the kids, your partner is gone; your friend, your confidant, your supporter, your cheerleader. The one who has your back, the one you are in this with and the one who holds you close and tells you that – together – you will figure this out! Besides being traumatized, I was so lonely in the face of these incredible challenges that I'd never thought I would have to work through on my own.

So through the tears, I stumbled into the house and grabbed the phone to see if I could find out where my car would be taken and what it would take to get it out of this predicament and back to me.

The next day I made the really tough decision to sell Bobby's motorcycle to get the car back. It was the quickest way to get my hands on that amount of money that was needed. That sweet boy never flinched. He loved his bike more than the air he breathed, but he jumped right in and did what had to be done for our family. My kids were living through things I never wanted them to know about, but there was no way to shelter them: we were all in this together, and we still are today!

I struggled to sleep for a long time after that experience. I never really stopped jumping up and running to the window when I heard a noise out front, until my car was completely paid off.

Luckily, my boss at the part-time job that I had just started the day I lost Joe let me come on full time. And slowly but surely, financially, we began to get back on our feet.

In the midst of everything we were trying to recover from, just two years after we lost Joe, my brother David died at only forty-two.

David had been left paralyzed at nineteen in a drunk-driving accident. When Joe died, David moved down to Georgia so he could be close to us. He had been building a home, and he just expedited his move.

He had so many health issues, but he ultimately died of a blood clot on his aortic valve, and we all waited with him as it broke loose and took his life. It was agonizing, and one more trauma for my little ones and me to find our way through: another death, another funeral, another loss.

CHAPTER 8
FINDING SUPPORT

As we began to join the living again, I was crystal clear that we all needed some support. I was struggling enough with my own stigma and comfort level talking about how we lost Joe, and friends had left us in droves. You don't really realize that this is what's happening; you just wake up one day and wonder where everyone went. So as the kids and I sat in seclusion, I knew I had to get busy and find some help.

A loss by suicide brings complications that you don't know to look for, or realize that it even matters that you specifically address. Our whole family was dealing with not only grief, but also trauma. For me, I tucked that trauma away and carried on. I had to be strong. Four kids were counting on me here!

At the time I didn't realize it, but there is a big difference between trauma and grief. And although you can recover from both, they have very different healing strategies.

I knew I was grieving, but I didn't really understand what part looked like trauma. Both grief and trauma, if not addressed, can impact your life continuously and forever – and not in a good way. I knew we were all on a journey to heal, and I was learning all I could so that I could keep us on a healthy path. We all grieved differently, but as long as we each kept moving forward, I knew we were going to be okay.

I had become isolated and alone. I knew that I had to get out and find others who had experienced this kind of loss. I needed help from people who understood how I was feeling and weren't afraid to hear what I needed to say and ask. The kids couldn't be my support system; although we were close and supportive, I had to find other adults who could help me.

I wanted to make sure that my kids wouldn't be marred for life by this event as well, and while I was struggling to keep myself on steady ground, I knew I had to get them to some kind of grief services also. So I started looking on the Internet for resources in my area.

The search brought me to the Link Counseling Center, which is also the National Resource Center for Suicide Prevention and Aftercare – and which, – luckily for me, is in Georgia. I found a listing there of SOS (Survivors of Suicide) support groups in Georgia and picked one that I thought would be closest to me.

As I dialed the number, fear began to overtake me and the tears began to flow. How could I speak my truth? What would they think of me? While the thoughts swirled in my head, a soft-spoken gentleman answered the phone. I said, "My name is Sheri and I recently lost my husband Joe to suicide." He expressed his deepest condolences and said that he was so glad that I had reached out for support. He was also a survivor of his son's suicide. He said that I was welcome to attend their group, and gave me those details, but he said, "There is a group in Roswell that is run by a woman who also lost her husband to suicide, and I think that you would connect to someone with a loss that is similar to yours." Giving me the number, he made it clear that if I didn't get an answer, or felt uncomfortable with that option, to call him right back and he would welcome me into his group. He made sure that no matter what, I would be supported.

I found my way to the leader of the Roswell group, who asked if I would like a home visit, which for me was a perfect choice to start this journey. The leader, and another woman who had also lost her husband to suicide, came out to visit us. This was a time for me to begin to share what had happened to us with people who understood, and listened, with no judgment.

They brought me resources and helped me to see how getting connected to other suicide-loss survivors would help and support me on this new journey. I really felt that they were there to make sure that I was going to be okay. It was a great transition to get me involved in the Roswell SOS group.

The other bonus that came out of that home visit was that this particular group leader had been leading some grief programs for kids at her church, and after meeting my children she put together a suicide grief program for them, and kids from three other families, who had recent losses of a parent by suicide. This connection changed the trajectory of my children's lives and put them on a path to heal.

After connecting with the support groups, I took all of the kids for a family session with the Link's Director, Iris Bolton, in hopes of giving us all a better understanding of how to survive this. Joe had been having a great deal of anger issues, and I was hoping for some kind of mediation to get my precious family working together. I was so desperate for everyone to be okay.

Iris was so gentle and sweet as she welcomed us, and talked to us about our loss. But as the questions and comments went around the room, my son Joe lost it, and walked out after some choice words. I was mortified. But Iris calmly told me that it was all right, and how everyone responds in a different way. As she walked us out, she said to me, "You have to let him grieve in his own way. Sometimes that way doesn't feel appropriate to others, but he will figure it out for himself." We could be on this journey together, but he needed to find his own way to walk it, his own way to mourn.

Years later, he told me that he had gone through a very dark time with his music, and it had helped him to work through his grief and find a way to honor his relationship with his dad.

We were blessed to find our way to those resources fairly quickly. It is so important for families who survive this type of a loss to get to resources as soon as possible. My children were so shattered that they never once said that they didn't want to go. Their leader didn't tell me what was happening in the group, but occasionally she would call with a helpful thought or broad update.

One night she called and said, "You know, Sheri, they know that you are crying alone in your bedroom and they don't know how to be with you in your grief. They want to be with you in your grief. And you need to help them to see that its okay to grieve and to cry." I was so surprised to hear this, but what a blessing she was to our journey, helping me to see that it was okay to cry with them or to show them that I was sad. I hadn't walked this path before, and I thought I was protecting my little ones. But she helped me to see how important it was that my modeling healthy grieving showed them that they could grieve also. It actually helped for them to be able to put their arms around me as I cried, just the way I did for them when they cried. It was something we had experienced as a family, and we had to walk together on this journey. That leader taught me to see so much about helping the children grieve – but also for me to grieve as well.

One day, about eighteen months after we lost Joe, she called me again. She said, "The children are doing so well. They understand, they love Joe; they know how much he loved them and that they played no part in his painful decision. They have put him in a good place where they can remember and draw on that. But they are ready to move on now, and to be like the rest of the kids." I smiled the biggest smile and shouted, "That's great!" It was such a gift to know that I had found the right support for the kids and there had been help for them. They were going to be all right! She told me that there will be times that still will be hard – graduations, weddings, and such – but that there will be remnants of grief that they have the skills to get themselves through.

Somewhere around that time I realized that I had to give in to where our feet landed, and for the kids, we had found a healing path that had guided them to hit the ground running and into life again.

But for me, although I had found my way to the support groups, and pushed myself out instead of hiding, my world was still feeling empty. Things were better with the kids even though they still had their moments, but I was still so very lost. I found lots of friends in the SOS groups who were always willing to support me in any way that I needed. They gave me something very different than what my friends and family who weren't survivors did. They gave me a clearer picture of what was okay and what was troublesome on my journey. They gave me a place to speak things that a non-survivor might not understand, and they never judged my story or my feelings. They gave me a safe place and a strong model for guidance on this journey. That is the gift of becoming a part of the survivor community. My survivor family truly saved my life. But even with that, I knew that I needed something more.

CHAPTER 9

A CHANGED LIFE, A NEW CAREER, A NEW DIRECTION IN MY JOURNEY

A loss by suicide changes everything. Everything you ever thought to be true was now in question. There is no area of your life that is left unchanged, which often leads to a search for meaning of some sort.

As my life got back on track, and the kids' lives were getting stronger, I began to feel the need for a more purpose-filled life.

Everything had become so petty; I needed something bigger that gave some meaning to this horrible tragedy. So I asked the SOS group leader to help me find some way to get involved.

She connected me with some volunteer opportunities with suicide prevention activities happening around the area, and specifically working with SPAN-GA (Suicide Prevention Action Network, Georgia).

The feeling of becoming active in this work was healing, and knowing that I was doing something to help others who had struggled just like Joe did, began to make sense. So I took on more and more, while still working a full-time job.

In the fall of 2005, the founders of SPAN-GA, Jerry and Elsie Weyrauch, asked me to take a leadership role in the organization. I remember feeling very surprised to be considered, and told Jerry that I didn't feel I was qualified to take the position. He made it very clear that I had everything that was required, and he knew that I would do a great job. "And besides," he said, "it will only be temporary." That was ten years ago! Jerry and Elsie would become my mentors, guiding me along the way, for many years.

Our organization had been given a line item in the Georgia Public Health annual budget to conduct suicide prevention projects around the state. Shortly after I came on as CEO, we began to work on a contract called, "The Georgia Rural Project." It was a great start for me, with a scope that allowed me to continue to work a regular job while I executed this contract. The essence of the project was to identify and submit a recommendation for alternative suicide prevention resources for youth in rural communities. Jerry had already brought on two renowned researchers with whom the organization had worked before, Dr. C. Hendricks Brown, PhD and Peter Wyman, PhD, to evaluate the potential programs that we would consider, and then develop a recommendation. So, I was to facilitate the organization and convening of a committee charged with assessing options and developing a model to meet the deliverables of the project.

Hendricks and Peter where "larger-than-life" professionals acclaimed in their field. I remember our first face-to-face meeting, and how nervous I was, waiting for them to arrive. We all sat at a large round table to begin our work. I guess I was nervous, because I told them, "I feel like a small speck amongst giants." They both laughed and said, "Ask our wives how great we are." I was so intimidated by their work and stature, yet they welcomed me to the table as an equal. They helped me to grow in my new career so much that first year and I'm sure they have no idea how very much they helped me. They became instant friends, who I love to run into on the rare occasion that our paths cross at the same conference or event.

The recommendation that came out of the Georgia Rural Project was so compelling that Hendricks and Peter began a pilot program almost immediately in our state, and then the state agency used it as a guide to apply for a very large GLS (Garrett Lee Smith) Grant. They were awarded the grant and received two rounds of grant funding, enough for six years. This work led my path to take an interesting turn, one that I certainly couldn't have ever imagined.

As I followed the suicide prevention activities around the state, and supported the work where I could, the folks from Public Health began to take notice and asked me if I would be interested in developing a grant proposal to work alongside the suicide prevention coalition-building efforts, and help communities learn to support families who had lost loved ones to suicide. It would involve helping community coalitions to develop survivor services in their area. I was shocked and flattered, and again, not really sure whether I had the qualifications to do this work. It certainly wasn't my lifelong experience, but they insisted they were comfortable that I would be a perfect fit.

This work had not been done before – and what an opportunity it was for me to start anew. So I set about breaking ground for this new work in my state, and as a model for others around the country.

Funny how life guides you where you should be, and when you should be there. I took on the role, and went on to create a successful four-point strategy for how to support survivors and create survivor services in communities throughout Georgia.

The first year I traveled extensively, going into each community and meeting people who wanted to be involved. Slowly the strategy began to reveal itself, and I became a light to show others how to help survivors of a suicide loss. I began feeling stronger and stronger in my role, and as I gained experience and confidence, I realized that I had found a way to keep Joe right with me and give meaning to his loss. Joe's story was helping so many others.

My work grew to be the Georgia statewide strategy for supporting families who had lost a loved one to suicide. Among many other things, we created a family grief camp, Camp SOS; developed presentations for law enforcement, community members, aging services, etc.; developed and distributed over 40,000 Survivor Support Purple Packets; and so much more.

As I traveled the state for many years, suicide prevention and survivor services began to be recognized as a critical need for all communities, and the work really began to grow.

One of my kids asked me, "Mom, isn't it sad to do this work?" My response was, "No, because if your dad's story can help one person – save one life – than we have given meaning to our loss and his life has had an impact."

CHAPTER 10
SO MANY LOSSES

So, as it happens, life goes on. My career continued to grow, thrive and allow me to do some amazing work in our state. But sometimes, we carry on not knowing what the traumas we have experienced have left behind to wreak havoc in our lives. Although things went back to a busy full life, those challenges can weigh us down in ways we may not even see.

Even when we think we have had more than our share, in our case, things continued to happen to challenge our progress – and especially, to test my own healing.

My first memory of loss was when I was fourteen; my Grandmother Moore was killed in a drunk driving accident. Grandma Moore was such a gift in my life. She was one of the kindest, most loving women, and she meant the world to me. When she would come and visit us, she often took me into New York City. We would get on the train in New Jersey and head to the city for a afternoon of shopping, dinner and the theater. It was such special time for me. I loved her so dearly, and when she died so abruptly I was completely crushed, and broken hearted for my sweet Grandfather who had survived the accident. He suffered for the rest of his life without her.

Her loss was so unexpected and painful that the funeral was filled with traumatized family members loudly sobbing and wailing. It was a hard situation for a child to deal with. The grief of the adults was so profound, that no one even considered what might be going on for the kids. This was my first exposure to such a traumatic loss.

At twenty-eight, I lost my father. Dad's loss was also abrupt and unexpected. Mom and Dad had retired and moved to their retirement home in Arizona. My family made the move with them. Five-days after we arrived, my Dad had a massive heart attack – and he died instantly.

I had been giving little Joey a bath, and as he skipped through the den on the way to his bedroom, he jumped over his Grandpa who was lying on the floor. My dad often spread out on the floor to watch television. The problem was, he was not pointed at the TV, but instead he looked as though he was headed to my mom who was asleep on the couch.

I dropped down to the floor beside him and rolled him over trying to get a response, all the while trying to wake my mother to call 911. I began doing CPR, but I think he was gone when he hit the floor.

It was such a significant loss, Dad was such a dominant figure in all of our lives, and his loss left a gaping whole in the family. We all struggled as we tried to move on. None of us understood the importance of mourning a loss, so in an effort not to upset Mom, we just didn't talk about it and carried on with life even though it clearly affected all of us.

But then years later after losing Joe and then David, and finally regaining our footing, in 2005, my mom passed away. A few years before that, she had been told that she needed heart bypass surgery, which could have added years to her time with us. But she had smoked all of her life, even with serious COPD and an oxygen cord resting on her face, the addiction continued to be in control. We were told that if they attempted the surgery she would never get off the ventilator, and no surgeon was willing to try. So it was just a waiting game as she went through those last couple of years. She had so many ups and downs through that period of time, when I was just barely hanging on myself. But she was my strength, my rock, through it all.

At one point she fell, which was the beginning of the end. Her health got worse and worse, and eventually she was put into an assisted-living home. She was close, so we could see her almost every day. But she knew her time was limited, and during the week of her eightieth birthday – after we'd spent many days sitting with her and holding her hand, thinking it was "her time" – she passed.

Losing Mom presented unique challenges in my life. It took me many years to identify that the trauma of losing Mom had begun a downward spiral for me.

My mom had been the person in my life who was always my safety net. She always caught me when I fell, much to the chagrin of my family. I know it must have seemed to them that she helped me more than she helped anyone else. But the challenges in my life had been very different than theirs. I envied that they didn't need her the way I seemed to. I hate that I may have caused her to direct her attention to me, especially if they felt that it took away from her time with them. It was never my intention, and it was hard to see then what I see now.

In my mind, I knew I would always be okay, because she was there. Even if I didn't have a need at the moment, I could count on her to be there when I did. The preceding years had been challenging with Joe, and with keeping life and my head above water. So losing Mom was more than just losing my mother, it was losing my feeling of safety. She had been such a dear friend, and a precious mom who wasn't well for the last few years of her life. She had needed me (and others) much more than I physically needed her. But in my mind, she was at the core of my safety and security. She made me and the kids feel protected through some very turbulent times. I'd had so many traumas throughout my life already, and her presence was my touchstone for knowing that everything would be okay. She was always there for me and gave me solace.

Within the next few years after her passing, I began to have mild panic symptoms. I called it "catastrophic thinking," where I would think that the worst was about to happen. Driving to Macon every month became a nerve-racking nightmare. I would drive down the highway, and as I approached a big truck, I would imagine that he was going to swerve into my lane, or his load was going to come crashing out of the side of the truck onto my car. Even small things became bigger – for instance, if I didn't tell the girls to be careful when they left the house, I feared that something horrible was going to happen to them. It was stressful, and it made my life way more challenging. I was beginning to feel a little "crazy".

I had thought that it was caused from losing Joe and all we had endured. But years later I began to put the pieces together and link it to my mom's death.

Losing Mom had shaken my foundation, and it came out in these reactions. Again, I didn't realize that this was trauma-related, or even seek help for it. It was just one more thing on my plate. I didn't know why – or even that I should reach out for help.

One day in March of 2008, I came home from a three-day conference to our traditional birthday dinner for my twin girls and my sister Mary. We always had a birthday dinner for all three at the same time, as their birthdays were a few days apart, and Mary, loved celebrating with the girls.

We had planned the dinner before I went out of town. So when we arrived at the restaurant, and Mary didn't show, we all knew something had to be wrong. She lived and breathed for my kids. She would never have missed this dinner. We called, but no answer. So after dinner, my son Joe and I went to her house.

The garage door was closed, but she was still not answering the phone or door. So I called my family in Florida, and we all agreed that Joe and I should break in. I called 911 to let them know, and then, with a big rock in hand, we smashed out the back door window.

My son Joe went ahead of me, protecting me from what might be there when we got to the top of the stairs. As we approached the landing, I heard him say, "Oh, no!" He could see her feet, and it was clear that she was gone – and had been gone for some time. We entered the room and he checked her pulse. She was cold and rigid, and her skin was bluish.

Joe was so precious and gentle. He said, "Mom, the police will be here in a moment. Take this time to be with her before they get here." He walked downstairs to meet the police, while I stood beside her, touching her cold hand and weeping uncontrollably.

At forty-seven years old, she should be getting ready to go on the trip she had been planning, and celebrating her birthday with us. She hadn't even called me to tell me that something was wrong. Why hadn't she called me?

I had been away for three days, so we pieced together what had led up to this moment and figured it had been maybe two days since she had passed. The coroner said that it looked like a diabetic heart attack, and he felt as though she had gone quietly in her sleep.

Her meds were scattered everywhere. She had recently been prescribed insulin, which she had never opened. Even the bottles of her pill version were everywhere... full. They didn't do an autopsy because they were pretty sure what had happened.

But yet again, I had found my baby sister dead, another trauma added to the list, and this one with a memory that would linger in my mind for a lifetime.

The stress of all of these major traumatic episodes was clearly affecting me, but again I just kept moving forward. I didn't know what else to do, although I did look for ways to help me deal with the panic responses I was still struggling with.

Within those next few years, I actually had what I thought was a heart attack four separate times, sending me to the emergency room, only to find out that it was anxiety. It was hard to believe that my mind could make me feel something so physical. My mind and body had gotten to a place where even though I was trying to manage my stress, when my psyche felt overloaded it would shut down and send me into a panic. I began to think I was losing my mind, and that I was weak.

After the third hospital visit in five years with what appeared to be yet another heart attack, I went to my primary-care doctor, who put me on the lowest dose of Zoloft. I had finally given in, and it was clear I needed some help. The panic attacks and catastrophic thinking began to subside. But there had been no signs preceding the attacks, so I was always in fear that another one could happen again, out of the blue, at any given moment.

Life began to get back on track, and once again I got myself steady and moving. My career continued to grow as I gained more knowledge and skills to support and grow the work: prevention, intervention and aftercare efforts; training, speaking and presenting; creating programs; starting a camp. The new life that this career had brought gave me strength and confidence, and the old Sheri was coming back and thriving. Finally!

CHAPTER 11

SURVIVING, THRIVING AND FLOURISHING*

The years that followed, were not all bad, as a matter of fact – they were really pretty good. The kids grew, and we went through girlfriends, boyfriends, baseball, ballet, theater, dance team, music gigs, proms, graduations, even a wedding and one of my greatest gifts: my first grandchild, Matilda.

I tried to give my kids a good life, and for them to never know that we struggled. The beginning was hard, but eventually we found our footing.

Bobby had struggled so after losing Joe, and after high school he became a bit stuck. He was going through some wild ways, and pretending that he didn't care, but I knew he did. One day, out of the blue, he came to me and said, "Mom, I want to go to college." I was shocked, but I of course said, "Great!"

He had already contacted the college to see what the process was, and soon a representative from UTI, Universal Technical College, came to the door to interview Bobby. It was so great to see him taking charge of changing his path, and he was determined. The representative was very impressed with Bob, as was I. He was clear what he wanted, and the gentleman told us what he had to do to achieve it. They happily accepted him into the program.

The school was not in Georgia though, so we would have to get very creative with scholarships and loans. But within weeks, Bobby was planning to go to Norwood, Mass to begin his college life.

There were so many changes happening with the kids, mostly good. Joe had gotten married, had a child, and sadly, divorced. But even though it was terribly painful, it was the right choice. He was and is a wonderful dad, who kept modeling love and stability to his little girl, even through the struggles. He was launching his music career and recording. He released his first album, *From these Seeds,* in 2008, and then *Tin Umbrella* in 2010. It was such an exciting time. During that time, he met his future wife, Calais. They dated for a number of years, and eventually, Joe planned a secret rendezvous. Katie and her boyfriend Josh would hide among the bushes to record him getting down on one knee and asking her to marry him surrounded by the lights of the Atlanta Botanical Garden Christmas festival.

The girls were doing great, "A" students, happy and social little beings. Around the time that Bobby went off to college, the girls graduated from high school with honors and also went on to college. Both got full scholarships and attended a wonderful university in Georgia, and then went on to graduate with full honors in college as well. Katie earned her degree in Studio Art, while Susie received hers in Math Education. It was a time of great pride for me as I watched all my kids flourishing!

Kate and Josh dated through College. After several years, he also planned a surprise rendezvous with all of their friends and Kate's twin sister Susie. They all traveled to Nashville, and on the most beautiful walking bridge, covered in twinkling lights, he got down on one knee and asked her to marry him.

Bobby had graduated from UTI with a degree in Diesel Technology with full honors, on the dean's list. He was so proud knowing that he was on a path to get a great job and be successful, and I was so proud of him! He went on to do some product-specific training in Arizona with

Cummins Engines. He loved being out in the town where he was born, Scottsdale, Arizona, but he had to come back home when he finished that training so he could begin to look for a job. It didn't take him long to find a Cummins location that wanted him, and he made the move to Savannah.

The job was a great one, but I worried so about him because the workforce was made up of men in their forties and fifties. He was working such long hours that it was hard for Bobby to find friends his age.

His first year was really lonely. I checked on him often, and we would Skype so I could see his face! He came home every month for a weekend. But after that first year, we didn't see him as often. He had finally met some friends his age, Scotti and Nic, who became his Savannah family. Life really turned for him at that point. And even though when he moved to Savannah, I had originally thought he would get some experience and then move back home, I soon realized that he had made a home for himself in Savannah, and he loved it.

After he got his motorcycle, he joined a riding club. Although Nic was always his best bud, the guys in the club were a brotherhood, a connection, a community, and that kinship changed Bobby in a really good way.

Our lives were overflowing with joy. We had survived, thrived and were even flourishing.

SURVIVING, THRIVING AND FLOURISHING*

CHAPTER 12
LOSING MY BOBBY

One day as I was getting off work, Katie called me. She said, "Hey Mom, one of Bobby's friends left me a message on Facebook and asked if I knew where Bobby might be, as he hadn't come back to work after lunch." He had left a number, so I told her to call him back and see what was going on. While she did, I went to Facebook, thinking if he had just wanted to ditch work for the day and escape for an afternoon ride on his motorcycle, he may have posted some pictures of scenes along the way, something that he often did as he rode.

What I saw when I got there sent pain and fear shooting throughout my body. My breath left me, and as I gasped, I knew I had to get into action. There was a news segment posted from the local midday Savannah news about a grave motorcycle accident on the 515. The young man who had posted it said, "Please don't let this be Bobby McGuinness." But I knew it was. I could see his bike in the photo, or what was left of it. I called his best friends, who started searching hospitals to find where he was.

They found him very quickly, and the word was to gather the family. My heart began pounding as I made calls to the kids and they all came running. I think we were on the road within an hour, for the longest drive of my life as we made our way from Woodstock to Savannah.

My mind was spinning. I'm sure all the kids were doing the same. No one knew what to say – we tried to think the best. As I thought through all of the possible outcomes, there were none that were good besides a full-out miracle. So I began to pray for that miracle.

After a long drive, and finding the hospital in the dark, we made our way to the trauma ICU. There were many of his friends waiting at 1:30 am for us to arrive, in hopes of seeing Bobby or at least getting an update, as no one would talk to them.

I had been able to speak with a nurse, who was caring for him, but she wouldn't give me much information over the phone; she said she wasn't allowed. But I told her that I gave permission for his friends to be with him. I didn't want him to be alone. And I knew his friends would comfort him, until I could arrive. She said that would be fine. But when we got there they hadn't allowed them to go in. I didn't want my boy to be alone; why hadn't she let them sit with him? He had to have been so afraid, and so alone, I thought to myself.

So we made our way to the door of the ICU where the nurses were located. We asked to see Bobby. The nurse who had come out asked what we needed, and she went to ask about him and where he was. When she returned, she escorted us into a smaller room to sit and wait for the doctor. We knew at that moment that this wasn't going to be good. Two doctors came in: a woman and a man. The woman doctor spoke. She said, "Bobby has been in a motorcycle accident and has had a "non-survivable traumatic brain injury." I will never forget those words. Non-survivable? What was she saying? Where was he? Was he breathing? What was going on here? I was in shock. The kids gathered close.

She went through the list of broken bones and blood-pressure challenges, but the only thing I remember was "non-survivable traumatic brain injury." They said he had not been conscious since the accident and that they had done everything medically that they could to assist him. They had even started his heart again at one point. They asked us if we wanted them to start his heart if it stopped beating again. I told her that the answer is YES; we couldn't make that kind of decision within five minutes of arriving and hearing this news. I told her that we needed the night. She had said that the neurosurgeon had placed a chip on Bobby's brain to track any activity, and by morning they would know more. So I asked that they give us until then to think through any medical decisions for him. It was so much to consume in a matter of minutes. They finally brought us to see him.

He looked like Bobby, but just sleeping. I put my hand on his face. His trim cut beard was so soft. I leaned over and kissed his head, telling him we were there. He had casts on his leg and arm, and all sorts of wires and tubes, including the one coming out of the top of his head that led to that chip. That one would be the one that would let us know if he was still in there, trying to get out. It was such a surreal moment, all of us standing around him: Joe and his wife-to-be Calais, Susie, Kate and her husband-to-be Josh.

How do we do this? There was nothing that could prepare you for a moment like this. I remember clearly so many tears, and thinking, as they dropped to the floor, how big they were as I watched them splash on the linoleum.

I grabbed his hand at one point, and it was blue. I looked at it again and held it, trying to set a memory of what it felt like inside mine: my baby's hand, my boy. I knew in that moment that he was already gone. I was thinking that the blood rushes away from the extremities to the heart in a last-ditch effort to survive. But I knew he was gone, that these machines were just keeping his body going. Really the hospital staff was just following protocol, placing the chip on his brain so they could tell us in the morning that there was no brain activity, and keeping him alive so we could say goodbye. I didn't tell the kids what I thought at that moment. They needed to have until morning. Let's see what the tests say, if there is any brain activity at all, because no matter what I felt at that moment, what if there was. It was just too soon to give up. We all spoke to him as if he could hear, and told him we would be back. We told him to fight, and we were fighting with him, and that we loved him.

We all headed off to the hotel we had found on the drive down. I wondered later, why didn't I stay with him? I wanted to, but the nurses had said we could have a few moments, never offering for any of us to stay. But honestly, I think I knew that he was already gone. And here we all were in the midst of another trauma, the biggest trauma of our lives. We needed to be together.

I'm not sure anyone had slept, but the next morning we got up and headed to the hospital to be there as soon as they would allow us in, hopeful for that chip to tell us there was some glimmer of hope that the doctors hadn't known. We arrived and his friends were there waiting, Scotti and Nic bringing donuts and a spirit of hope trying to lift us up. They would only allow two of us in at a time to see him, so Susie and I headed to his room, only to find the doctor there working on him. It was hard to watch

Bobby's limp body flop around while the doctor roughly tugged at him. The nurse came over and asked us to wait in the waiting room until the doctor was done. So we did. But then someone came out and got the family and brought us into yet another small room. We were now with people who seemed to be pastors or chaplains, who waited with us for the doctor to arrive.

When the doctor came in, he very coldly told us that Bobby had passed. His heart had given out one last time, and they couldn't revive him. I wondered why the doctor had been so rough while Bobby was so fragile. And why they hadn't waited until we saw him one last time that morning, before pushing his frail body to its breaking point.

They let us spend some time with him that morning. Saying goodbye. I knew he was gone, had known he was gone. But there was my boy. I touched his beautiful face again, trying to embed one last memory, one last touch. I would never touch my precious boy again. How could this be? I saw some of his hair on the bed where they had shaved his head to put the chip in, and I grabbed it and wrapped it in a tissue. Not sure why. This was surreal and so permanent. I guess I was grasping for one last thing to remain. The room filled with sobs and tears, and so much pain, as we said goodbye to our Son and Brother and Friend.

CHAPTER 13
LOST IN A HURRICANE

My mind was spinning; I couldn't even compose a thought. The pain overwhelmed me. I wondered if I might die in that moment, and wished that I would. My heart could barely stand this. My body felt as though it were vibrating and might explode.

Trying desperately to draw on that proactive person that I always was, I thought, "So now what? What do we do? Where do we go from here?" Within hours, we had gone from hearing that Bob was hurt, to being told he was gone. It felt as though I was in a bad movie; it just didn't seem real.

We hadn't eaten – not that we were hungry, but we had to make plans. I didn't know how to do this. I didn't know what to do next. But we decided to go somewhere that we could sit and talk.

As we walked out of the hospital, my cell phone rang. It was my sister Susan, calling from the local airport. She and two of her sons had headed to Savannah when they heard of Bobby's accident.

I was in such shock. As I answered the phone, all I could say was, "He's gone." She said, "What?" I repeated, "He's gone Susan." We both cried. Susan said, "Where are you? Where can we meet?" I told her we were leaving the hospital and that we would meet at a restaurant near the hotel.

Susan was my angel that day, and in the days to come. Her boys, Michael and Stephen, were such a blessing in the face of such pain. Each of them was supporting us and being so careful to let us lead the decisions in a confusing, devastating time, and doing whatever it was that we needed of them. I was and always will be so grateful for them.

I remember seeing her face as she pulled up in the restaurant parking lot. I couldn't speak. She held me so tight, and all I could feel was how broken my heart was, and how grateful I was that she was there with us. We stood there for what seemed to be an eternity. There weren't words to express what was happening. But she was there, and her boys were there, and my kids were there, and together we would all figure this out.

My kids were being so strong; I know they where trying to hold Mom up. But this was such a crisis for us all. Joe had Calais there to help him, and Katie had Josh and Susie had Katie and Josh both, and we all had each other. It was such a time of coming together. We held on to each other to get through this horrible nightmare.

As we sat and tried to gather our thoughts, discussing what our next steps should be, Josh said to me, "I have my big truck, so I could tow a trailer back to

Woodstock. We could get Bobby's place packed up and get it all home for you now. That way you wouldn't have to find a way to get back to Savannah right away." With all of the people we had with us, everyone agreed that it really made good sense.

So, Calais jumped in and said she would find a place and go get boxes and tape, and Josh lined up the trailer, while Steve and Mike searched for Bobby's keys to let us into his apartment. They weren't in his clothing, which had been given to us at the hospital, so they must have still been with his bike, or what was left of it. So the guys headed to the car impound where they had taken the bike to see if the keys were there, and luckily they were.

Once we got word, we all met at Bobby's place and started to pack it up that evening. Kate and Susie stayed close to me, making sure I wasn't overwhelmed by going through all of the pieces of his life. Everyone tried to keep it light as we laughed at what a bachelor kept in his refrigerator. It was hard going through my boy's things, thinking of all the pieces of his life that he had worked so hard to create.

The next morning, Josh went to get the truck, and many of Bobby's friends showed up to help us load it up and get him home. He lived on the third floor with no elevator. Between Joe, Calais, Susie, Kate, Susan, Michael, Steve, Nic, Scotti and other friends including Rachel, the girl he had been dating, I'm not sure how we would have accomplished it without all of them there that day. Physically and emotionally, their presence made me feel Bobby close by.

As we were packing and loading, I realized that Bobby hadn't been a very materialistic young man. Everyone wanted something to remember him by, but he really didn't have much. Interestingly, when holidays came around he never needed a thing or wanted much. He loved his family, his friends and his motorcycle, maybe not in that order. He was a simple soul who had such a clear perspective on life. He was a good man who had such integrity, and even though he was quiet, once you got to know him, you knew how intelligent and really deep thinking he was.

When he would come home to visit, we had such incredible, deep conversations, sometimes until three in the morning. He questioned many things and had really suffered the loss of his dad. He wondered how life could be so unfair, so unequal. But he knew that goodness was at the core of his being, and so that was who he was.

Together, we got Bobby's things packed and ready to head home. We stopped at his work and got his tools, and hugged the necks of his work buddies. Then we got on the road from there. Susie arranged a storage area across the street from our subdivision so we could go right to it when we hit town. That way I could take my time, and sort through his things in a more organized way when I was ready.

It was hard leaving Savannah. Hugging the necks of all his friends, his Savannah family. Although I knew his body was on the way to Woodstock, it felt as though I was leaving him behind.

The days that followed, planning his funeral and saying goodbye, hurried by in a haze of grief and sadness. I vaguely remember an endless line of visitors waiting their turn to give me their condolences, and each hug brought an onset of more tears. There were friends who loved Bobby, friends who loved and supported me, and even friends of my other kids all came to comfort and love on us; so many loving shoulders to cry on.

My sister Susan and my friends were very close by, watching to make sure I wasn't overwhelmed and needed them to step in. And although I was definitely overwhelmed, there was some solace in holding on to the people who cared about him.

Finally, we had gotten to the end of the receiving line. My sister gathered my kids, and moved us into the main room as the service was about to begin. It was a hard moment for everyone, but Bobby's closest friends got up and spoke in the most eloquent way, remembering him, honoring him, loving him, and even creating some laughter in the packed room, which was exactly what Bobby would have wanted.

The day before the funeral, Joe wrote a song about how he was feeling. He sent it to Susie so she could show it to me, and make sure that I was ok with the words. It was so beautiful that even though it made me cry, he just had to share it with the people who loved Bobby so, which was clear by the packed chapel at his service.

The song was called, "Invincible," and he sang it with such passion from his heart as if he was speaking right to Bobby.

INVINCIBLE
You're goin too fast and
you're gone way too soon,
The sweetest man I ever knew.
If I could pull down a star, for all the
times you made me laugh,
I'd have the whole evening sky in the
palm of my hand.
Right here in my hand...

Why you in such a hurry?
Where you going so fast,
With that big smile on your face as
you give it the gas?

LOST IN A HURRICANE

And with the throttle wide open,
you go by in a blur
Thinking that you're invincible,
I wish you were,
Yeah, I wish that you were

You made everything better,
just by being around,
I can think of you laughing,
To lift me up when I'm down.
And I'm mad at the whole world,
cause it keeps carrying on.
Doesn't it realize that my
favorite part's gone,
my favorite part is gone.

Why you in such a hurry?
Where you going so fast,
With that big smile on your face as
you give it the gas.
Yeah with the throttle wide open,
you go by in a blur
Thinking that you're invincible,
I wish you were
I wish that you were
Wish that you were.

Did I tell you I love you?
Well I hope that you knew.

Choosing Hope, Finding Joy

More than you can imagine,
little brother I do,
You know that I do.

Why you in such a hurry?
Where you going so fast,
with that big smile on your face as
you give it the gas.
Yeah with the throttle wide open,
you go by in a blur
Thinking that you're invincible,
I wish you were
I wish that you were.

Well life is so short; it goes by in a blur,
Thinking that you're invincible,
I wish that you were

There wasn't a dry eye in the room, as he tenderly sang the words of his amazing tribute to the brother that he loved so.

Our family and friends got us through those next weeks. But, the silence on the other side of the funeral brought me to a place of great darkness. My Uncle Gordon and Aunt Betty had come to Bobby's funeral. I was so surprised as it was a very long drive, and I hadn't seen them in years. But they had lost my cousin, their precious Claire, many years before – and felt that they should come. For a long time after the funeral, Aunt Betty would text me with messages of love and support. Just that small contact was so comforting in the midst of the darkness. I knew she understood where I was.

The kids and I made a deal that if we ask, "Are you are okay?" we acknowledge it is relative to knowing that *nothing* is okay, because nothing *was* ok.

I had told Bobby years before that he must think of me every time he gets on his motorcycle, and drive it safely always, because I couldn't live without him. Joe now repeated that statement to me, and he made it clear that *they couldn't live without me,* so I had to find a way through this. And although I knew it was what I had to do, after so many years as the "grief expert," I really wasn't sure that I could.

CHAPTER 14
THE DARKNESS SETS IN: A DIFFERENT KIND OF LOSS

The days that followed were hard, to say the least. The kids, and my friends and family all kept close tabs on me. I don't even remember much of what went on in those early months – except that day after day, I sat in my chair in the den, looking up at the street at the end of our driveway, picturing the world moving on as though nothing had happened – while I sat paralyzed in the darkness. "Don't they know that the world has ended?" I wondered.

Everything was so different than when I lost my husband Joe. Back then, there wasn't an option to focus on me. I had kids to raise and support through this loss. I had to be a role model for them of how to survive this. But now, I felt as though I was the child and my kids were taking care of me, when I know they needed me also. I couldn't seem to draw on the skills that I knew so well to help others through grief. I could barely function myself.

Also, when I lost Joe, so many people had retreated, leaving us to figure it out on our own. But now I was surrounded by so many who loved me. That should be a good thing, and don't get me wrong – it was! But the pain was so severe that I needed to be in control of my every movement. When well meaning friends would try to get me out of the house or keep me busy, it felt like being on Mr. Toads Wild Ride at the amusement park – out of control and frightening. Other times I felt so alone and I was grateful for their presence. I knew it didn't make sense and wasn't good to isolate, but I wasn't feeling safe. Home was definitely my safe place, so I stayed as close as possible. Sometimes the support made me feel out of control, in a place where I needed the control so badly.

Many of my friends would text me every day, which was a great way to stay connected and feel cared for while still letting me feel a bit more in control. They were keeping an eye on me from afar. Their connection was my lifeline. But ultimately, I knew I couldn't just hibernate.

The kids kept me going, never judging me, even though I was acting a bit extreme at times. I'm not sure how I would have made it without them. One small text and they came running. Katie and Susie would come in and sit with me, putting their arms around me, holding me until I was calm. Joe would talk to me and help me sort through my thoughts, some of which were not very rational. He was so patient, and he never gave up on me, even when I seemed a bit delusional.

All three of them worked together, and they didn't let me fall. It felt like such a role reversal from when I lost Joe. And I didn't have the power to do anything but accept that help. Even though I am so grateful, and these kids are the best kids ever, somehow it made me feel weak and useless, and even, occasionally, completely crazy.

So I sat in that black hole, deep in the darkness. It was as dark a place as I have ever been, with no windows or doors. The sheer pain of not being able to fathom that my boy was really gone kept me paralyzed. For a while, I just didn't let myself believe it was true – it just couldn't be possible. I would think to myself that he was just in Savannah enjoying his life. But that darkness has little space for hiding from the truth. It just holds you there consumed by pain, loss, disbelief, and the only path out is to face it all.

THE DARKNESS SETS IN: A DIFFERENT KIND OF LOSS

My thoughts continually ran to pictures of him running down the street laughing, riding his skateboard or four-wheeler, or just hugging me. I tried to remember every single memory of his life. I didn't want to forget one single one. But the more I remembered, the greater the pain I felt. The hole just grew larger and larger, and darker and darker.

I tried to push myself to go out when I could, to work when I should, but the blackness always called me back. I could tell that I was getting a little stronger, and that I didn't always cry all day every day – just most of the day, and then it went to some of the day. But even as I got steadier, I had moments where I got so close to the edge, I felt that I could easily just jump off. I knew I was in trouble.

I had moments where I could see how someone could step over the line of sanity and no longer be able to make a choice from a rational mind. Those moments visited me more and more, and that scared the heck out of me.

Three months after we lost Bobby, Katie and Josh were married. I think that the planning and preparation was a bit of a positive distraction for me, because I wanted to make sure nothing interfered with Katie's beautiful wedding day – including, and especially, my grief. And I think mostly it didn't. But Katie had asked Bobby to walk her down the aisle in the place of her dad. So she had to create a new plan, which was hard, but it worked out really well. Her brother Joe had been asked to marry the couple, so he switched roles and walked her down the aisle, and my nephew Stephen stepped in and performed the ceremony so beautifully. It felt so personal and close that we were all a part of this moment. It really was amazing. We definitely missed Joe and Bobby, but the day was nostalgic and wonderful, and joyful, as we welcomed Josh and his family into our lives.

Many days came and went, and without distractions, I went back to the dark place. When Bobby died, the kids and I decided that he would have wanted to be cremated like his dad. I work in the field of grief, and so many of my dear survivor friends had kept their children's ashes. So, not knowing the right choice for such a fast decision, I too decided to keep them for now. I knew I could make other plans down the road. I just didn't want to make a rush decision that I would be sorry for. So I would wait until I was sure.

For now, they would stay in the den. I knew that it wasn't healthy to build a shrine around them, but they were there, with his motorcycle helmet. As I would pass by, my hand was drawn to touch them both: sometimes for a second, sometimes for longer. At first it was comforting to be able to touch him. But I slowly began to realize that it kept pulling me into the darkness again.

Not Bobby, but the pain that the black leather urn represented. No matter how I tried to survive this, the darkness of his death just kept pulling me back in. And although his helmet felt like a friend and represented his life, his love and his joy; his ashes represented such darkness, and I couldn't get away from it, reminding me with every touch.

So on his birthday, almost seven months after we lost him, I decided to make plans to bury his ashes next to his dad's. The moment I made the decision, I knew it was right. I knew Bobby wouldn't want his ashes to be a painful reminder of this tragedy every day, and I knew he would want to be beside his dad.

Susie went with me to the cemetery that day, and we made the arrangements to have a celebration of his life on the anniversary of his death, January 16th, 2015. I wanted to wait for that date so that we didn't add yet another date to dread each year. So doing this at the one-year mark sounded like a good plan.

There was something of a relief that day that I made my mind up and I knew what to do. And I know it was the right thing for the kids and me. It's such a personal decision, and there is no right or wrong choice. It was what was right for me.

The holidays were hard: his birthday, Joe and Calais's wedding, Thanksgiving, Christmas. We had never spent family time without him. The kids wanted it to be the same as every other year, and I think that they thought that's what I needed. I didn't know what I needed. But it was hard that he wasn't there with us. Still we made the best of it, and as Bobby would have wanted, we laughed and loved each other.

The kids did a great job of bringing him into the holiday with us, remembering him and making sure that I knew that we would never forget him.

I struggled so with the idea that the kids might feel that I thought Bobby was more important than each of them, which certainly wasn't true. But I could feel the hugeness of Bobby being missing in my life, and it seemed to be larger than my love for any one thing that was left behind. The guilt ate me up as I struggled to make sense of it. They were taking care of me, and I struggled with that. I love them all so much, but the loss was just so overwhelming. It was just so hard to find the balance in that much pain. But I continued to look for it.

I did realize somewhere on this path that I clearly had an innate resilience that kept me fighting to keep going. Even though I really just wanted a tree to fall on me so I could be with my baby boy, that desire to survive was still intact. I knew my other three were here, and still needed me, even though I was in shambles. We were in this together, and they never ever let me forget it!

CHAPTER 15
ARM CHAIR ANALYST/LEARNING TO LEAN

Complicating my already-convoluted journey, I knew way too much about grief and loss, and I was constantly analyzing my thoughts and reactions. If I cried, I was out of control. If I didn't cry, I was in denial or felt guilty. I knew all the things I would say to others, but they didn't seem to be working with me. It was so hard to just let myself grieve. Somehow I envisioned myself being this perfect role model for grief, though even I knew that it was ridiculous. But the expectations were there nonetheless.

I was under pressure to get back to work. Most of that pressure was from myself, though the work did have to get done. But after losing Bobby, I was in no condition to be a role model for anyone, or to help anyone else grieve. I was a mess – and how could I help anyone when I couldn't even help myself? I kept analyzing where I was and how well I was doing, and it was never right. So I questioned what I could possibly say to help someone else on this journey.

I had gotten strong enough to throw myself back among the living again, but not really strong enough to stay focused for long periods of time. My work still needed to get done; so wherever they could, my team took the lead. They are an amazing group of people who are more like family than colleagues, and whom I hope will always be near me.

Not long after we lost Bobby, the date for Camp SOS was fast approaching. Camp SOS is a grief camp for families who have lost a loved one to suicide. It had been a dream of mine to develop this camp for SOS families, and through a crazy series of events, a camp opportunity fell into my lap. I picked it up and ran with it to my team!

We had started the camp three years earlier, and it had grown to be the most amazing model of peer-to-peer support in suicide grief and loss for all ages, six to ninety-six! It was the one element of our work that we all loved the most! So camp would definitely go on.

I was so fragile, and I really had no business going at all. But I was the glue that had pulled the camp together. Although, I was the Camp Director, and took care of the structure of executing the camp, the team took charge of the rest. They led the activities, facilitated the groups and provided the most awesome experience for our survivor families, all the while protecting me from too much exposure to new loss that they knew could re-traumatize me. They took over the key roles and I stayed in the background, as we pulled off an extremely successful camp.

As for the rest of my work, I focused on prevention and the other things that didn't get me too close to new survivors. As I tailored my workload to meet my grief and my emotional needs, I could feel other things happening within me. I knew my own worth in the field. That gave me strength – but pushing myself to keep going wore me out, and it made me tired of the mundane parts of the job.

After I lost Joe, life had led me to this career. It was my gift after that loss. It was a great gift that I had taken up, and I rose to the challenge. I value it so, but there was something burning at me. After losing Joe, I found purpose that helped me on my grief journey. Knowing that left me wanting to find a new purpose: something that gave meaning, or kept Bobby's light shining around me. I was sure there would be healing in that purpose. But as I searched for it, I just became more and more frustrated, and more frantic to find something that just wasn't there to be found.

There was way more than grief going on for me. At first I thought it was because I now had lost my child, and although I do think that was a big part of it. I don't think it was all of it. The more I thought about it, the more I felt certain that there was something more going on here than just grief, as if grief wasn't enough!

This was such a different loss, with such a different grieving process. I remembered how Joe's early childhood trauma had been revisited when he lost his dad so horribly. I began to wonder if some of my past was making it harder for me to want to find hope.

I could see that I had really led a trauma-filled life, beginning very early. But each and every one of those traumas was culminating in a very challenging grief. Although I would say losing Bobby was definitely the hardest loss, I began to see that it was being complicated by the past traumas in my life.

I thought that maybe I couldn't manage this on my own. So, not knowing where else to go, I went back to see the counselor I had seen when Joe was struggling. One thing I do know is that not every counselor or therapist is a good match. And this first attempt was disastrous, even though I had seen him before. We had known each other for too long, and our conversation was as much about his challenges as mine. I was way too frail for that.

There was too much of a comfort level there, and I needed it to be about me. My kids made me promise not to go back, and even my therapist friends said to find someone else. So here I was again, on my own, trying to figure it out.

CHAPTER 16
REACHING OUT FOR HELP!

Before I lost Bobby, I had experienced those serious anxiety attacks. The traumas of my past were already affecting me, even back then. But after his loss, my mental and emotional well-being was pushed further than it ever had been and I just couldn't take any more.

One day, I got away for lunch with a dear friend who worked with me in the field of grief and aftercare, and who also happens to be a therapist. In my work, I know lots of them. But this person was definitely more than a colleague; she was also my friend, who cared deeply about me, and I about her.

I remember seeing her walk through the door of the restaurant that day, and I began to cry. There was something safe and nurturing about her, and I just needed a safe place to let myself be vulnerable. But being in this field, I was embarrassed that I was so out of control of my grief. Apologetically, I asked forgiveness for my inability to carry on much of a conversation.

As we talked, she comforted me in such a tender way. She gave me the space to feel exactly what I was feeling, and she let me cry. But the greatest gift she gave me that day was to tell me that she thought she was seeing signs of trauma in some of my responses. She asked me if I wanted her to give me a referral for a therapist, and that I really should find someone who specialized not only in grief, but also in trauma.

I was almost relieved for her to speak those words. I certainly trusted her opinion and valued her recommendation, but also to feel a confirmation that I was right: there was more going on here.

I knew I couldn't fall prey to the stigma that surrounded acknowledging the need for and seeking help! I had to use the resources that I had recommended to so many others in need. I had to trust the words I had been speaking for years, and I gratefully accepted the referral.

And besides, I knew I was in trouble. I just wanted to get better, and I knew some of my responses were extreme, so I was ready for wherever she directed me.

The therapist she referred me to was great. And although I know it can be hit or miss, and you have to keep trying until you find the right one, this therapist was a perfect match for me. I felt a trusted connection with her from the start, and as we began to work together there was an instant comfort and safety. This was one of the best decisions that I made along this new part of my journey, and I was grateful that I could afford it. There had been plenty of times in my life that I couldn't have.

At first it was hard, and I cried a lot! But it was a safe place where I could just let go, and I always felt better when I left. Slowly I began to share, and I started to move forward.

From the start, I made it clear to the therapist that I didn't want her to psychobabble me. I wanted tools and skills. I needed to know that I would be empowered to one day be in control of my journey, and manage my triggers with those tools. And that's what she gave me!

CHAPTER 17
TRUSTING THE PATH

Somewhere along the way, my mind had decided that there was a direct link between recovery and purpose, so I continued to search for what that could possibly be. Day after day, I sat in faith that it would be revealed to me if I just hung on. But Bobby's death had been so senseless that I just couldn't find a purpose, because there was none to be drawn – or so I thought.

I had found my way to therapy, and I knew that was a big step. But it certainly wasn't an instant fix. As a matter of fact, I was in such pain those first months and that first year, I couldn't imagine help or relief arriving soon enough.

I thought many times about dying. I never had a plan, but if a car had run me over or if I just didn't wake up it would have been okay. The hole I was in was so big and so dark that I couldn't see many possibilities.

I felt such guilt. I didn't want to leave my other kids, but Bobby's death was so immense that it consumed my thinking. I couldn't see anything else; I couldn't seem to get perspective. I am a smart woman but I couldn't sort this out. I didn't see an end to this pain – ever. And it was greater and darker than any pain I had ever felt.

Starting therapy didn't mean that all of a sudden all was right with the world, but it was a huge step. Just having a safe place to cry for an hour was a good start, and then slowly becoming an active partner in my grief and recovery.

I began to see that although I did know a lot about grief, trauma was another story. And I really needed to understand how it was manifesting in my life. Therapy was helping me see the bigger picture, and begin to recognize it.

One of the greatest things that losing Joe had taught me was to trust the path. We certainly need to call on our wisdom to make decisions in life, but when circumstances put us in a position where wisdom is challenged, sometimes we just have to trust.

My sanity clung to my confidence, determined that no matter what, we were going to be okay. And that confidence didn't let me down. It actually fortified my resilience and kept me going. I think they call it "blind faith." And it was all I had to hold on to.

Looking back, I can see that without really even acknowledging it, somewhere along this journey I chose hope. Even though I couldn't see it, maybe didn't even want it, I chose hope – and I continue to choose hope.

CHAPTER 18
LETTING GO,
A NECESSARY CHOICE

After the New Year, on January 16th, 2015, we all came together to honor Bobby in a short service at the cemetery. I had already had his ashes buried, and the beautiful marker placed, next to his dad's.

My dear nephews and their families, Bobby's Savannah family and dear friends who lived close, all came to join the kids and me to remember him. In the midst of such darkness, it was a positive day of remembering my boy, and it brought me great peace. I didn't realize it at the time, but my grief changed on that day.

The decision to bury his ashes had helped me to separate the continual, painful trauma of Bobby's death from the wonderful memories of the twenty-seven years I was blessed to have him with me. It allowed me to have my home be the place that represented his life. The separation let his light surround me again, instead of serving as a constant reminder of his loss.

The blackness didn't completely leave me, but I had found a light bulb in the black hole, and I could begin to see that there was a glimmer of light at the top. This was a turning point for me. I was still grieving, but there was an acceptance, and a peace, that began to support my journey in a very different way. I knew I had to keep my eye on the light – and it would lead me where I needed to be.

CHAPTER 19
BOBBY'S WISHES

I remember telling my counselor one day that I needed to find that purpose that I so desperately sought. Somehow I honestly thought it was my only way out of this horrible place. I thought it would help the pain subside.

She said she understood, but asked me how long it had taken after Joe's death before I found my way to the work I do now. I remember my response was determined and sure. I told her, "Five years." Then, through my tears, I said, "But I can't spend five years at this level of pain." I knew I wouldn't survive. I was hanging on by a thread, and there was no way I could do it for five years.

Still, I knew that finding purpose after Joe's death had helped me, so I was sure that it would help me now. But that purpose couldn't be motorcycle safety or something to do with riding. Bobby would kill me. He loved that bike maybe more than he loved me! Just kidding, but it would dishonor Bob, and all he loved, for me to go in that direction. So what do I do, how do I have a way to keep Bobby close with me every day in a positive way, the way my work had done with Joe? That was my challenge, and my frustration.

As I had thought that finding purpose would save me, when I realized that there was no purpose to be found, I began to believe that I wouldn't survive this. My life raft had never arrived – there was nothing to hang on to. I knew that to stay stuck in this horrible pain and give up my life to it would diminish Bobby's life. He would never want my life and the other kid's lives to be ruined, and for me to live the rest of my years in horrible pain, wailing and mourning.

One day I couldn't stop thinking about what Bobby would want. His best friend had told me that when Bob heard that he was estranged from his dad, Bob had told his friend the story of losing his own dad, and that he would give anything to have him back. Bob had told him that no challenge is worth that divide – and said that he hoped his friend would think about repairing that relationship.

Bobby was such a caring young man. He didn't always say much, but when he did, he was straight up and not afraid to say exactly what he thought. It was never with malice, but if Bob said it, it needed to be said. He was kind, and would never purposely hurt someone or be cruel. As a matter of fact, he would go out of his way to help someone who needed him. He was a respectful young man to a fault, someone you could trust with your life, and I couldn't have been more proud of him.

He definitely was a momma's boy, but in a good way. He loved his momma more than anything else. He thought I was the greatest mom who had ever lived, and even though I'm not sure that's true, he always made me feel that it was. He valued the lessons in life that I had taught him, and believed that he was a great person because I had taught him to be. One day, after we lost Bobby, Katie and I were talking, and she began to cry and said, "Mom, who's going to listen to your wisdom?" I laughed – but in a weird way, it felt true.

The more I sorted through all the wonderful things about him, the clearer it became that I had taught him to be true to himself, that anything is possible, to follow where his spirit led, and to be all that he had within him to dream and achieve. And that is exactly what he would want for me! He was so proud of everything that I did, personally, my work and my mission. But most of who I was when the kids were young, and what made my own spirit sing, had been put in the closet long ago while I fought to find a way for us to survive. Out of necessity, it was stuffed so far in the back that I didn't even know it was there anymore. But the epiphany was clear.

To honor Bobby, and to keep his light shining, I had to be the best me I could be. I had to find what my spirit needed – and share it with the world. That is who my Bobby was, and what he would want me to do.

An overwhelming need to be creative began to taunt me, and I made my spare room into an art studio. I started quilting and painting, anything that filled my yearning. One day while I was at my therapy session, we were talking about that need to be creative, and I told her that after Joe died I had wanted to write a book, and had started it, but life got in the way and I never finished it. She got this excited look on her face and said, "Wow, the other therapist in my group just came back from a Writers' Retreat, where she wrote her book in a weekend! Would you like me to get some information about it for you?" A feeling of fear struck me, but all of a sudden I was intrigued. Where I normally might have shied away from putting myself out there, my spirit was pushing me to check it out.

I went home and pulled up the website and learned as much as I could about it. I began to get really excited at the prospect – and soon I had registered, bought an airline ticket and set up my hotel accommodations.

A few weeks later as I was preparing for the retreat, I was doing an assignment on my computer that they suggest you do before heading to the writers' retreat. It was in the form of a YouTube video, and the instructor was walking us through a clearing exercise. Something strange happened as the video played. The instructor asked that we sit with our feet on the floor, and close our eyes. Then, with outstretched hands, to picture someone coming toward us – and ask them a burning question that we would like answered. I was questioning if going to the retreat was the right choice, or if I was in over my head. So, as the music played, I imagined that someone was approaching. Within just a moment, I realized that it was Bobby, with the biggest smile across his face. As he moved closer, his arms reached out and grabbed my shoulders. He looked me in the eyes and said, "Mom, you've *got* this, you *know* what to do!"

I knew at that moment that he was guiding me to where I needed to be. He wanted me to find myself again.

CHAPTER 20
A LIFE OF TRAUMA; THE POWER OF RESILIENCE

Truthfully, fulfilling Bobby's wishes wasn't as easy as it may sound, and it was certainly more complicated. No epiphany would take away the grief and loss. But it did give me hope. I began to investigate who it was that I was looking for. To begin with, to find myself again I had to overcome some of the challenges that a life of trauma had left behind. I had to look at how it was really affecting my life. Why was I having these dramatic responses? Which part was grief over losing Bobby, and which were overreactions caused by past traumas?

I had been through so much in my lifetime, from the childhood abuse to the many losses with varied degrees of impact, and Bobby's death had brought them all running back. At this point, I had even been diagnosed with not only trauma, but also PTSD.

With the help of my therapist, I began to dissect them and see the bigger picture. She was giving me the tools to manage what was happening. I was learning what might trigger the reactions, and what to do if it happened.

I was amazed to learn how trauma works, and I began to see the places where it had altered my thinking, and affected my choices, all throughout my life. It had grown to be more in charge than I wanted it to be. It was interesting to learn that it is actually your mind trying to protect you, but unfortunately it is using faulty logic to make decisions around that protection. And it would take time and work to retrain my thinking. The good news was that it was possible. There definitely was hope!

I often wondered to myself, why had I been resilient and not Joe? Why did he give up and I kept fighting? As much as I have been through, I have always found my way to survive – and even thrive – again and again. I have kept going in the face of so many challenges, where many people might have given up. So where did that come from? And why couldn't Joe find that within him? Why couldn't he see hope, and find the strength to keep fighting?

As I look back at both of our pasts, I could see where I had been given many skills and tools. My parents had taught me unconditional love; they had shown me that failure was only a lesson waiting for you to learn, and that there are always second chances, new paths – and hope!

But Joe's young life had been so interrupted by the years of abuse, that even if there were skills to be learned from his parents, his ability to grasp them would have been severely distorted. He had a sense of self-survival; but it wasn't based in resilience, it was based in fear.

He had no skills or tools, so his coping choices were most often inappropriate or harmful. And although he kept looking for answers, he didn't have the ability to see a vision for the future that was based on trusting that path. He had no faith in the path. He had no faith in his abilities. He had no self-worth or value in himself. All of these served as devastating blows to possibility and hope.

CHAPTER 21
THE TRUTH ABOUT DEPRESSION, GRIEF AND TRAUMA

After the loss of a loved one, it is important to learn as much as you can about what they were struggling with, as well as learning about what your own journey from this point might look like – including understanding grief and grief support, and all that this may entail. Knowledge is definitely power. And honoring your need to grieve is paramount.

Your journey will be unique – different from everyone else's – but there are skills and tools to learn along the way that are universal. So I want to share a few key points with you.

Grief is a real thing. It can be very physical at times. It frequently lasts a long time, even a lifetime. But luckily, it changes along the way and becomes bearable. We need to learn the tools that will help us to navigate this journey in a healthy way, or we may get stuck, or travel in the wrong direction. We aren't a nation that honors grief. We are quick to think that we need to be over it. In reality, grief is a healing process, it never leaves us – it just transforms into something we can live with.

Grief is nature's way of helping us cope, and it's a natural response to loss. And loss is a relative thing for each individual person. Someone who loses a best friend can be just as affected as someone who loses a spouse. And there are even other types of loss that can be debilitating: losing a job, an identity, a home, or a marriage. There are many types of loss that can impact us and cause grief and trauma. Almost everyone will experience grief at some point in his or her life. But when there is trauma associated with the loss, it can be much more difficult.

Grief responses and trauma responses can look similar, but trauma responses are much more intense. And trauma can make it harder to process the complex emotions that we are already feeling.

We can often heal from grief on our own in time. But if we suffered a traumatic loss, the emotions of that grief can be too overwhelming for us to resolve on our own. Losing a loved one in a shocking, unexpected way such as in an accident, or by suicide or homicide, may have traumatic consequences. Trauma makes grief harder to resolve. It can impair your ability to manage your grief and keep yourself moving forward.

If there have been other losses, trauma, anxiety or depression in a person's life, it can be even more difficult for them to manage another blow. When this happens, the symptoms of their grief can become almost unbearable. This is a point where they need to get professional help, as it isn't something that they can navigate on their own.

Although it is possible to grieve without being depressed, the sadness of grief and clinical depression can be two very different things. Depression can affect our recovery, and it needs therapeutic support.

I know this all sounds very scary. I'm saying it, though, to point out that grief itself is hard enough – but if that grief begins to take the form of depression, or to look like trauma or even PTSD, it's best to seek professional help. These are not things that we can move ourselves through, and even if we ignore them, they will be affecting our lives in one way or another indefinitely.

It takes some effort to find the right support. Try more than one therapist or counselor if you aren't comfortable with the first. Educate yourself about the various types of therapies available, specifically for grief, trauma and PTSD. If a counseling center doesn't offer a certain kind of therapy, they may not suggest it, so you have to be your own advocate. Stick with it – with no preconceived notion of how long it might take to "get better."

Stigma should not guide our chances to be healthy and whole!

There are so many people who do not have access to or funds to pay for therapy or counseling. For those people, don't give up on the possibility. Keep searching, and advocate for yourself. There are many places that may be able to help you find those resources – for yourself or for your children. Go to your local NAMI Chapter, check with your community service board or family connections, or call you state behavioral health department and ask for help in finding resources!

For those who can afford to be in counseling, – it is such a gift – use it!

CHAPTER 22
CHOOSING HOPE

Hope is really a choice. I understand that there are times when the black hole keeps us from seeing the hope, sometimes burying it so deeply within that we give up. I know that Joe had gone to that place where he thought hope would never find him. He had fallen so deep into the black hole that he had nothing to hang onto, no glimmer of light.

It's a fine line, and once you find your way there, it requires someone's help, lighting the way back to hope, which isn't always as easy as it sounds.

There were many days when I was really scared I would go far enough into the black hole that rational thinking would leave me. I wouldn't be able to see the possibility of hope. I could tell I was really close to that place.

But before you get deep within the blackness, hope still remains a choice. In those moments, I definitely knew that it was possible to lose sight of any hope. I was fighting desperately to stay away from that edge. I think that may have been the one place where knowing too much about grief helped me.

It brought me to a place where I felt that I had three options:

1. I definitely could decide not to choose hope and to end my life.
2. I could choose to suffer endlessly for the rest of my life, but that choice would probably <u>ruin my family's lives as well.</u>
3. And then, last but certainly not least, I could choose hope – and continue to

reach for that hope until it pulled me back into the light.

For me, the third option meant having faith, and trusting my path, even though I couldn't see where it would lead me. I clung to that for dear life until I knew it to be true. And one day, that's exactly what happened.

Choosing hope is a commitment to do whatever it takes to find joy in your life again, even though a big piece of you is missing.

Bobby would not want me to be unhappy, and destined to grieve and suffer for the rest of my life. And although that is harder than he would think, I knew I couldn't give in to the darkness.

After we buried Bobby's ashes, I had chosen hope. It wasn't a black or white "I'm done grieving" kind of thing. But the light came back on, and the sun started shining again. I know it was not only because I had given myself a place where I could visit him, but also because I chose hope that day. That didn't mean I stopped grieving or that there was no pain. It just meant that I had pointed myself in the direction of hope.

Loss is a hard thing always, and losing a child is something you never get over. I know that. There will always be tears, and some days are still very sad. But choosing hope means you continue on the path, you watch to make sure you are still on the path – and you look for ways to give meaning to the loss, to remember, to honor, to keep your loved one's light shining.

Everyone lands on the path or takes this journey after loss, and there are many ways you can choose to travel it. Without knowing, you can end up staying in the back hole. Honestly, even as you go back to work and go through the motions of living, you can still be in the black hole. You really need to think about where you are, because it's easy to fool yourself.

Look at the ways to honor your journey, while keeping your grief healthy. Surround yourself with good friends who will talk with you about your journey. Often they may see "stuck-ness" where you don't, and be okay with that. Each family grieves differently, and each person within the family grieves differently. That's all right. And the children need to work through their grief as much as the adults do.

Don't expect members of your family not to feel something just because you hate that they do. Let them feel it, let them express it. Honor it, and hopefully one day they can let it go and move on.

Sometimes your "stuck-ness" can impair the whole family's ability to move forward. Remember that there is no one way to do this, but ultimately, you are the one responsible for watching and checking your own progress along the way. Keep yourself moving forward, and make sure that your choices aren't hurting yourself or others.

Choosing hope is a choice to find options to help you heal. We can't change that our loved one is gone, but we can choose, step by step, the path we take for ourselves. From that moment forward, it's a long journey – so it's not just one choice on one day. It is a constant haggling with hope.

For me, choosing hope meant giving into the challenge and pain that was so much bigger than I was. It meant accepting that the traumas throughout my life had affected me, and they had culminated in a huge blowup on impact at the loss of Bobby, making my journey even more challenging – as if I needed anything more.

For me, I needed my family and friends, but I also needed a really strong mental-health professional to help me navigate things, and to trust her and stick with her even when I disagreed or didn't understand. That was my roadmap to finding joy again.

CHAPTER 23
FINDING JOY

I don't ever want to diminish the pain and heartbreak that loss brings. I know what the journey is like, and I walk it every day. Although much of your own personal journey may be without conscious thought or planning, rather just walking one foot in front of the other, especially at the beginning – when you are ready, be open to joy again. If you keep moving forward, you will know when that moment arrives.

I'm not saying that it's easy to choose hope and find joy. There is a feeling of betrayal, when joy begins to return, which feels as though we have let go of our loved one – or maybe even forgotten. I have been at that crossroad many times, and I know that it is a hard moment. At some point we begin to identify the heart-wrenching pain as all we have left, and we cling to it with desperate abandon.

We have to come to the place to face that the last few moments of our loved ones lives were not all that we have. We also have all of the wonderful years of memories and life that we shared with them. Granted, this is not the outcome that we wanted, but it is what we are faced with.

I know that neither my husband Joe nor my son Bobby would be happy to see me sitting in that darkness. I didn't have much choice though, particularly early on, feeling stuck in such incredible pain and wailing with grief.

I try to remind myself of that every day. It doesn't mean that I don't miss them, think about them daily, and even cry for them. It just means I have found a way to think about them much of the time with a smile and a warm feeling inside my heart. They were my gifts for the years that they were with me. And now I can value and be grateful for that.

I promise you, taking that step will not erase your loved one from your life and your heart. Instead, it will show you a new way to keep them close – a happier way.

After I realized that I had chosen hope, I pointed myself toward finding joy again. I tried to convince my newly married daughter that a new grandbaby would be just the joy I needed, but to no avail.

So as far as joy goes, it's a bit elusive at the moment. I have to be kind to myself and remember that grief is a journey. As long as I'm looking for it, joy will find its way to me again. Some days it feels pretty far away – but seeking a full life that is connected with others, and doing all the things that continue to remind me to keep choosing hope, will also help me find the way to joy.

There may be new ways that joy can enter my life, ways I'd never have thought of. A new grandbaby would be nice, but it could also come from new friends, reconnections, new projects – or even a new book! But one thing I'm sure of is that I choose hope – and I'm determined to find my joy. I see glimmers, so I know it's possible. And that's good enough to keep me searching!

Grief doesn't really ever leave you. It changes as time goes by, and as you decide how you want to let it affect your life. I see Joe in my work everyday. It makes me smile to know that I have shared Joe's story to help someone else. I see him in my children's faces. I hear him in the music that they play.

I see Bobby everyday, telling me "You *got* this mom, you *know* what you need to do!" He is my inspiration, and my heart – which is where he will always reside. I hear him in the rumble of a motorcycle as it passes me on the highway. I can hear him laughing as the bike passes by. I see him in my other kids; I see him in his best friends: Scotti and Nic, Drew and Kristen, Brett; and

I see him in my precious "Great Baby" Abram Keith.

A wise young man named Nic once told me that Bobby and his dad Joe will both live on, because we will make sure to carry them forward and remember them always – and they will live on in our stories and memories. When you set down the devastating pain of the loss, and remember and honor the precious life, and Choose Hope – all things are possible – Even JOY.

BONUS CHAPTER 24
A SURPRISE ENDING

As I sat in my chair at the Tom Bird writers' retreat, I wrote the final sentence in the previous chapter – which I *thought* was the last line of *Choosing Hope, Finding Joy*. I knew I had finished the first draft of my book. I stopped, closed my notebook and set down my pen with great commitment.

But the next day a surprise happened. I was walking around the beautiful Sedona resort with the biggest smile on my face, greeting everyone I saw, and feeling a part of this family of authors with whom I had been sharing this amazing experience. I felt great accomplishment and pride, in a time where self-doubt and fear had overtaken most of my waking moments. I also felt a sense of purpose and value. That day I realized that my life had significantly changed. A peace had come about me, even in the midst of so much pain, and a sparkle glimmered from my eyes.

As I hopped into the elevator heading up to the second floor, alone for a brief moment, I realized my writing had given me a rush, a thrill that felt so fulfilling. It had stirred up a desire that was not only burning then – but one that I knew it would continue to burn. As I glanced at my reflection in the steel wall, I let out a gasp. The smile on my face stretched from ear to ear. Raising my hands to my chest, I marveled as a quiet whisper left my lips..."I have found my joy!"

The tears began to run down my face as I realized that although a grandbaby would bring me a very special kind of joy, the greatest joy of all was that I had found myself.

I had found my joy – and it was within me all along!

CHAPTER 25
RESOURCES

Anyone who has found their way to this book, and needs help finding support, may check out the following resources. If you are a survivor of a suicide loss, if you have had another type of loss, if you want to learn more about loss and grief, if you think you or someone you know is having some issues related to trauma, these resources can provide a helpful start. The best advice I can give anyone is to learn what you (or your loved one) are dealing with.

Knowledge is power, and understanding changes the perspective that is so desperately needed to reach out for help. We shouldn't ever be ashamed to get the help we need.

Stigma should not guide our chances of being healthy and whole.

If you don't see the resources you need, please contact me – I'm happy to share! Peace...

RECOMMENDATIONS, RESOURCES AND REFERRALS

GRIEF – There are many resources for grief that you can find online, nationally or within your state. Here are some that we want to share with you.

Family, Children and Teens –

The Dougy Center, The National Center for Grieving Children & Families
This resource is for any type of loss.
help@dougy.org
Portland, Oregon 97286

Hello Grief
http://www.hellogrief.org/resources/
The Hello Grief website has some great information, but the link below brings you to a list of resources and you can choose your own state and see what is available there.

National Alliance for Grieving Children
https://childrengrieve.org

KidsAid
http://www.kidsaid.com

The Moyer Foundation
http://www.moyerfoundation.org/nbrg/defa
ult.aspx
*This is a listing of grief organizations and
grief camps all over the nation.*

A Child in Grief
http://www.newyorklife.com/achildingrief

Compassionate Friends
http://www.compassionatefriends.org/
home.aspx

AAS – American Association of Suicidology
http://www.suicidology.org

TAPS – Tragedy Assistance Program for
Survivors
http://www.taps.org
Caring for the Families of our Fallen Heroes

NAMI – National Alliance on Mental Illness
http://www.nami.org/

MHA – Mental Health America
http://www.mentalhealthamerica.net/

RESOURCES IN GEORGIA:

The Link Counseling Center – National
Resource Center for Suicide Prevention and
Aftercare
www.Thelink.org
*The Link has counseling services and grief
programs for children and adults including
support groups for survivors of a suicide
loss.*

Department of Behavioral Health and
Developmental Disabilities, Office of
Prevention, Suicide Prevention Program
http://dbhdd.georgia.gov/

SPAN-GA Suicide Prevention Action
Network, Georgia
www.span-ga.org
www.campsos.com
*SPAN-GA is made up primarily of
survivors and does a wide variety of
things, much of which focuses on survivor
services. They are the founders of Camp
SOS, a family camp for those left behind
after a suicide loss.*

GSPIN – Georgia Suicide Prevention Information Network
www.gspin.org

This is a website for information; among other things, you will find a listing of all the SOS (Survivors of a Suicide Loss) groups in Georgia.

*For a national listing of SOS Groups, go to www.afsp.org

CAMP SOS
www.campsos.com
Camp SOS is a family weekend camp for families who have lost a loved one to suicide. This camp was started in 2011.

NAMI- GA
http://namiga.org/

MHA - GA
http://www.mhageorgia.org/

TRAUMA –

The National Child Traumatic Stress
Network
http://www.nctsn.org/resources/audiences/
parents-caregivers/what-is-cts/12-core-
concepts

*This site has lots of resources, including a
list of successful treatments for trauma.*

SAMHSA – Substance Abuse and Mental
Health Services Administration
http://www.samhsa.gov/child-
trauma/understanding-child-trauma

APS – Australian Psychological Society
https://www.psychology.org.au/publications
/tip_sheets/trauma/

The ACES Study
http://www.acestudy.org

GoodTherapy.Org
http://www.goodtherapy.org/learn-about-
therapy/issues/ptsd

Types of therapy used for trauma and PSTD

SEXUAL ABUSE RESOURCES:

National Sexual Violence Resource Center
(NSVRC)
http://www.nsvrc.org/

Center for Disease Control (CDC)
http://www.cdc.gov/ViolencePrevention/sexualviolence/resources.html

RAININ
https://www.rainn.org/get-help/local-counseling-centers/state-sexual-assault-resources

American Academy of Child and Adolescent
Psychology (AACAP)
http://www.aacap.org/AACAP/Families_and_Youth/Resource_Centers/Child_Abuse_Resource_Center/Home.aspx

OTHER REFERENCES:

The song "INVICIBLE" can be found on Joe's website,
www.joemcguinness.net
As well as his latest album is available for free download.

Sheri McGuinness, Author/Trainer /Presenter
www.sherimcguinness.com
Check out *The Healing Heartbeat Blog*

Mending Hearts Consulting
www.mendingheartsconsulting.com

* The Phrase – "Surviving, Thriving and Flourishing" was coined by Iris Bolton. Thank you Iris ☺

EVERY BODY NEEDS A CHEERLEADER

There are many people that I would like to acknowledge, but far too many to name everyone. My extended family: Susan, Dave, Bob, Jane, Kevin, Marc, Erin, Michael, Laura, Stephen, Jordan, Jacob, Michelle, and Becki, have supported me and the kids faithfully – I love you all dearly. There were many others who have walked with me as I found my way to this new beginning. My SPAN-GA Board (past/present): Diane, Tracie, Karen C, Richard, Sherry, Carol, Becky, Alex, Iraida, Jerry and Elsie. You are all amazing dedicated warriors for our cause, and luckily for me, also my dear friends. Additionally, my close colleagues/friends: Karen O, Sally, Maureen, Michelle, Pat, Barbara, Betsy; all my Survivor Family, and my Suicide Prevention Family (who it would take me another entire book to mention all by name). I am grateful to work and walk beside you all each day, and be a part of this amazing community in action.

Special thanks to my awesome teachers and cheerleaders! This book would not have seen the light of day without the incredible energy, love and support from Tom Bird and my Charlie Coyote Team!

Last, but certainly not least, I want to thank my mentor and friend, Iris Bolton. I remember attending the AAS Healing Conference years ago. You were up on the stage in a panel discussion. As you sat waiting your turn to speak, your face was beaming with joy. Even as the other panelists sat, their faces still with languid stares – yours never lost its radiant smile. As I watched you that day, I thought, "I want to be just like her. I want what is within her that allows her to always radiate positive light and joy, and give others hope." Iris, thank you for always being a guiding star for me to follow.

52967738R00117

Made in the USA
Lexington, KY
16 June 2016